MYSTERY BABYLON

When Jerusalem Embraces The Antichrist

An Exposition of Revelation 17 and 18
By Chris White

A special thanks to Charles Cooper

Table of Contents

Preface and Introduction

Even among dedicated Bible scholars and teachers, there is a wide range of views about the identity of Mystery Babylon, ranging from very allegorical to literal.

Some very popular teachers assert that Mystery Babylon is metaphorical and that it is not an actual city, but rather that it is symbolic of something else, possibly a world pagan religious system and/or a world financial system.

In counting the characteristics given to Mystery Babylon in Revelation 17 and 18, I have found over ninety distinct qualities given to it by Scripture. In this study, I will show that there are explicit biblical interpretations of most, if not all, of these ninety characteristics, and that by comparing Scripture with Scripture, we can come to a more biblical identification of Mystery Babylon.

The angel in Rev 17:18, while interpreting John's vision, mentions that the woman is a city.

> *"And the woman which thou sawest **is that great city**, which reigneth over the kings of the earth." - Rev 17:18*

Mystery Babylon (MB) is referred to as a city eight times in the book of Revelation, and many of the things that happen to it in the narrative seem to be talking about a literal city. For instance, the city is burned down and the smoke can be seen from the nearby sea, merchants sell items to it, it experiences famine, and many other factors which we will soon see cause many to believe that MB is in fact a literal city just as the angel said.

Those who see MB as a literal city have proposed several candidates for the identity of the city over the years including:

1. Rome or Vatican City. Many early reformers saw MB as Rome. Somewhat ironically, the Catholic church also teaches that it is Rome on the Vatican website[1] though it is referring to ancient pagan Rome, where the Protestant reformers would say that it was the Rome of the Catholic church.

2. Some suggest it is the actual city of Babylon in Iraq. In this scenario, they say Babylon will be rebuilt in the future.

3. Mecca or some other Arab cities have been proposed. This view has been especially popular recently.

4. The City of Jerusalem. This is the view that will be defended in this book.

5. There is a long list of other less popular candidates, New York being one example.

I believe Mystery Babylon is the last days city of Jerusalem. I chose my words very carefully in this description. In other words, I believe it is the Jerusalem of the end times where, according to Daniel 11:45, the antichrist sets up his headquarters.

According to this view, the people of the city of Jerusalem will promote the antichrist as their Messiah and as the one true God, thereby committing the ultimate abomination, the ultimate harlotry. Not only that, but they will promote him and entice the world to follow them in their worship of the Man of Sin (Rev 17:2).

We know that the antichrist will choose Jerusalem as the place to declare himself to be god (2 Thes 2:4, Mat 24:15, Dan 11:31-32). And we know that the greatest religious persecution of all time, which is prompted by the Abomination of Desolation will happen in the city of Jerusalem, according to Matt. 24:15-21. So we already understand that there is a relationship between the antichrist and the city of Jerusalem, but few of us have put all the pieces together to understand the significance of the antichrist's apparent focus on Jerusalem.

Too often people look at the "woman who rides the beast" and try to define her in terms of what we have already seen in history, as opposed to what Scripture says we will see in the future. That is the primary reason people miss this, because, as we will see, it is certainly not because of a lack of biblical support.

For instance, Rev. 18:24 says: "And in her was found **the blood of prophets**..."

We don't even have to speculate as to what city the prophets were killed in, as Jesus says it is impossible for a prophet to be killed anywhere except Jerusalem!:

> *"The same day there came certain of the Pharisees, saying unto him, 'Get thee out, and depart hence: for Herod will kill thee.' And he said unto them, 'Go ye, and tell that fox, behold, I cast out devils, and I do cures today and tomorrow, and the third day I shall be perfected. Nevertheless I must walk today, and tomorrow, and the day following: **for it cannot be that a prophet perish out of Jerusalem. O Jerusalem, Jerusalem, which killest the prophets**, and stonest them that are sent unto thee; how often would I have gathered thy children together, as a hen doth gather her brood under her wings, and ye would not!'" Luke 13:31-34[2]*

This idea is repeated by the Lord in other places, as well. For instance, He tells them that their fathers killed the prophets and they hypocritically built their tombs. (Luke 11:47). In Matthew 23, He names Zechariah as such an example who He mentions was killed near the temple. He says that they will be held accountable and judged for the blood of all the prophets ever killed:

> *...The blood of all the prophets, which was shed **from the foundation of the world**...*

If the "blood of the prophets" is found in the city of Mystery Babylon, it is strong evidence in favor of it being the city of Jerusalem.

Jerusalem is specifically called a "harlot" hundreds of times in Scripture and always in a spiritual context, that is, the spiritual prostitution of following false gods instead of the one true God, and killing His prophets, etc.

Just a small sampling of this is in Isaiah 1:21:

> *"How is the faithful city become an harlot! It was full of judgment; righteousness lodged in it; but now murderers." - Isaiah 1:21*

Ezekiel 16 is entirely about this subject, and it starts out by saying:

> *"Again the word of the LORD came unto me, saying, Son of man, cause Jerusalem to know her abominations..." - Eze 16:1-2*

He spends the whole chapter saying things like:

> *"But thou didst trust in thine own beauty, and playedst the harlot because of thy renown, and pouredst out thy fornications on every one that passed by; his it was. And of thy garments thou didst take, and deckedst thy high places with divers colours, and playedst the harlot thereupon: the like things shall not come, neither shall it be so." – Eze 16:15-16*

Jerusalem is constantly warned in Scripture that if they do not turn from their "harlotries" they will be judged. As we go through Revelation 17-18, we will find that the specific judgments Mystery Babylon gets are the exact same as the ones promised to Jerusalem because of her spiritual harlotry.

This idea that Jerusalem is as a harlot, and also has children or inhabitants that are harlots, is what is meant when Revelation says that the "Woman" is the "mother of harlots" – the harlots are the inhabitants and Jerusalem is the mother.

I think that much of the confusion comes from the fact commentators want to put in the word **ALL** there: "the mother of **ALL** harlots," as if MB was the source of all bad things from the history of the world. But that's not what the text says. Mystery Babylon is "The mother of harlots" which is a figure of speech referring to the idea that she has harlot children, or inhabitants.

Like many others, I used to think the "Woman" was Rome or the Vatican, and I hope that like me, when we look closely at the verses about the "seven mountains," you will see why I see this interpretation, held by so many, is grammatically and contextually impossible. But we won't have to wait until that section to see that that particular interpretation is on shaky ground.

I also used to believe that it was referring to an allegorical amalgamation of the world's occult religions or financial system. You will see that that view requires a deliberate departure from the plain and simple meaning of the text. It also goes against the angel's own interpretation of this "Woman."

This imaginary "ALL" we discussed earlier makes people think that they have to have Mystery Babylon account for all the evil in the world, past, present, and future. So they go looking, in the past or in the present, for the most evil thing they can think of and that's pretty much how they come up with their interpretation – whatever the most evil thing is in their paradigm, is what MB will be to them. It's not a coincidence therefore that all the books about MB being some aspect of Islam showed up after 911.

The strength of going verse by verse through this difficult section of Scripture is its thoroughness. As I mentioned before there are over 90 characteristics of MB in these verses, and if you have the correct interpretation, all 90 should line up with your view.

Going verse by verse and line by line (also known as an expositional study) might be the first time some of you have heard that Scripture has things to say about MB that don't line up with your current view of it. I hope you will get as much out of reading it as I have researching it. This study will give me an opportunity to teach some of the most complicated aspects of the antichrist, as well as the city in which he chooses to set up shop.

At the end of this book you will find a section called **Answers to Common Objections**.

John's Vision of the Woman and the Beast

(Rev 17:1)

And there came one of the seven angels which had the seven vials, and talked with me, saying unto me, 'Come hither; I will shew unto thee the judgment of the great whore that sitteth upon many waters:

This first verse connects us back to the previous chapter (Chapter 16) where the seven bowls were being poured out. The seventh bowl is the judgment of Mystery Babylon, the very thing we will be studying. So let's go back and read that passage first:

> *"And the seventh angel poured out his vial into the air; and there came a great voice out of the temple of heaven, from the throne, saying, 'It is done.' And there were voices, and thunders, and lightnings; and there was a great earthquake, such as was not since men were upon the earth, so mighty an earthquake, and so great.* ***And the great city was divided into three parts, and the cities of the nations fell: and great Babylon came in remembrance before God, to give unto her the cup of the wine of the fierceness of his wrath.*** *And every island fled away, and the mountains were not found. And there fell upon men a great hail out of heaven, every stone about the weight of a talent: and men blasphemed God because of the plague of the hail; for the plague thereof was exceeding great." – Rev 16:17-21*

As is so often the case in the Book of Revelation, it will now, in chapter 17, zoom in to take a closer look at this great city whose judgment has just been foretold. This is a pattern seen very often in the book of Revelation and Scripture in general. For instance, in Revelation 13, it breaks from a chronological narrative to zoom in on the character of the antichrist and False Prophet. This same thing happens in chapter 7 where the chronology of the seals breaks to tell us more about the 144,000 and the "great multitude," and again in chapter 11 with the two witnesses.

Here it's no different. After telling us of the destruction of the "great city," it will now zoom in to give us more details about its character. Those details will continue for two whole chapters in this case, and they will be the focus of this book.

"And there came one of the seven angels which had the seven vials, and talked with me "

This is one of the seven angels in charge of the seven vials/bowls. The angel takes John aside and will begin to show him more details about the judgment of the "Great Whore."

It says here that she **"sitteth on many waters."**

This is not left for us to guess its meaning, as the angel will later tell us what this phrase means:

> *"And he saith unto me, 'The waters which thou sawest, where the whore sitteth, **are peoples, and multitudes, and nations, and tongues.'"** - Rev 17:15*

We can combine this with verse 18 which says:

> *"And the woman which thou sawest is that **great city, which reigneth over the kings of the earth." ** - Rev 17:18*

We see that this is a city that might be the center of a world empire of some kind. It will be the chief city in that empire or system. It is the seat of authority that the world government and world religious system comes from.

We will also see in Revelation 11:8 that Scripture specifically identifies the **"great city"** as Jerusalem. This would be consistent with Daniel 11:45 where speaking of the antichrist it is said:

"And he shall plant the tents of his palace between the seas and the glorious holy mountain…"

(Rev 17:2)

with whom the kings of the earth committed fornication, and the inhabitants of the earth were made drunk with the wine of her fornication

"the kings of the earth…"

Fornication

So what is this fornication? Revelation 19:2 states,

> "…the great harlot who **corrupted** the earth with her **fornication**…."

To corrupt (phtheiro, in the Greek) in this case means "to cause the moral ruin of.."

The terms "harlot," "whore," and "fornication" are used very frequently in the Old Testament, and only in a minority of the cases is it referring to actual sexual fornication. In a vast majority of the cases, it is used to describe the worshiping of false gods, *especially* in reference to Israel.

This is even the case in the famous story of Hosea the prophet. Hosea was told to marry an actual prostitute, but this was intended to be a symbol of God's relationship with Israel who committed spiritual prostitution by worshiping other gods.

Hosea 3:1 explains:

> *"Then the LORD said to me, 'Go again, love a woman who is loved by a lover and is **committing adultery**, just like the love of the LORD for the children of Israel, **who look to other gods and love the raisin cakes of the pagans.'"**

13

Spiritual harlotry is one of the most attested to symbols in Scripture. When God refers to harlotry or fornication and it is obviously symbolic, He makes it clear that it is spiritual harlotry achieved by the worshiping of false gods.

One example that illustrates this well is here:

> *"Wherefore, **O harlot**, hear the word of the LORD: Thus saith the Lord GOD; 'Because thy filthiness was poured out, and thy nakedness discovered through thy **whoredoms** with thy lovers, and with **all the idols of thy abominations, and by the blood of thy children, which thou didst give unto them....**" - Eze 16:35-36*

Here it is speaking of the practice of Israel sacrificing their children to the god Moloch, as well as the worship of idols of false gods.

We find another good example in Jeremiah 3:6:

> *"The LORD said also unto me in the days of Josiah the king, 'Hast thou seen that which backsliding Israel hath done? **She is gone up upon every high mountain and under every green tree, and there hath played the harlot.'"***

Here again we see harlotry made synonymous with the worship of false gods. The term "high places" is referring to the altars that would be made to false gods, and "under the green tree" was also a common place of false worship. This combination of terms is actually referring back to Deuteronomy 12:2:

> *"Ye shall utterly destroy all the places, wherein the nations which ye shall possess served their gods, upon the high mountains, and upon the hills, and under every green tree..."*

The inhabitants of the earth were made drunk with the wine of her fornication

The kings of the earth are committing fornication with her, but **the inhabitants of the earth** are **made drunk** with the wine of **her** fornications. The earth is drawn in to worship the beast by her own intense worship of him. We will see this more clearly when we study Rev 18:3.

I believe this is best understood as the city of Jerusalem promoting the antichrist not just as their Messiah, but also as God himself. They will be instrumental in the promotion of the worship of antichrist to the world. We see as we progress that the world during the reign of antichrist will do religious service to him, bringing gifts from every nation to worship him. This verse is saying that the world will be enticed into fully worshiping the antichrist by the great city and its inhabitants who lead the charge.

So you can see what it means here – she herself is committing this fornication, and the world is **made drunk** by it; and they themselves also commit the same fornication.

(Rev 17:3)

So he carried me away in the spirit into the wilderness: and I saw a woman sit upon a scarlet coloured beast, full of names of blasphemy, having seven heads and ten horns.

So here we are introduced to another crucial character in this unholy drama – **the scarlet colored beast "…full of names of blasphemy, having seven heads and ten horns."**

This is the exact same beast that is described in Revelation 13, which is almost universally agreed to be a description of the antichrist.

> *"And I stood upon the sand of the sea, and saw a beast rise up out of the sea, **having seven heads and ten horns,** and upon his horns ten crowns, and **upon his heads the name of blasphemy.** " - Rev 13:1*

It's important to understand the basic symbolism in our current verse; the "great city" (the woman) is **riding** the antichrist (the beast with seven heads and ten horns).

This does not mean that she is in any way in control of the antichrist. We know this because later on, in Rev 17:16, the antichrist actually turns on her and will destroy her.

She, however, believes she has found a true husband and her king in the beast.

>*"..she saith in her heart, **I sit a queen, and am no widow**, and shall see no sorrow." - Rev 18:7b*

Sadly, she is mistaken, and she will be utterly destroyed by the one that she calls her king and her husband.

Being **"full of names of blasphemy"** is an important description of the antichrist, and his speaking blasphemy is referred to in various places: (Rev 13:1-6; Dan 7:8, Dan 7:20, Dan 7:25, Dan 11:36; 2Th 2:4.)

A few examples of the type of blasphemy of the antichrist can be found here:

>*"And the king shall do according to his will; and he shall exalt himself, and magnify himself above every god, and **shall speak marvellous things against the God of gods**, and shall prosper till the indignation be accomplished: for that that is determined shall be done. Neither shall he regard the God of his fathers, nor the desire of women, nor regard any god: for **he shall magnify himself above all.**" - Dan 11:36-37*

And here:

>*"**Who opposeth and exalteth himself above all that is called God**, or that is worshiped; so that he as God sitteth in the temple of God, shewing himself that he is God." – 2Th 2:4*

Having seven heads and ten horns.

We will speak more in depth of the **seven heads** and **ten horns** when we discuss verses 9 & 10, but I believe they are speaking of the different occasions in history in which the spirit of antichrist has manifested itself in the form of human kings.

As we will see, John says of these **seven heads**:

> *"...**they are also seven kings**, five of whom have fallen, one is, the other has not yet come, and when he does come he must remain only a little while." – Rev 17:10*

One of the heads, I believe the seventh one, which is the one John says is yet to come, will be the antichrist who will receive a mortal wound and yet live.

Back in Revelation 13, when John is talking about this seven-headed beast he says the following:

> *"And I saw **one of his heads** as it were wounded to death; and his deadly wound was healed: and all the world wondered after the beast." – Rev 13:3*

The beast that MB rides is the spirit of antichrist that in the time of the writing of Revelation had already manifested itself in the form of kings six times in history, but one of them, the last head, was still to come in the future. We are also told in Rev 13 that one of these heads, which I believe to be the one yet to come, for reasons I will explain later, will be mortally wounded and will come back to life. This is the beast that MB worships instead of the true God.

(Rev 17:4)

And the woman was arrayed in purple and scarlet colour, and decked with gold and precious stones and pearls, having a golden cup in her hand full of abominations and filthiness of her fornication

"Arrayed in purple and scarlet colour..."

This particular phrase: **"purple and scarlet,"** occurs twenty-nine times in the Old Testament, all of them in the book of Exodus; the only other time it occurs is here in Revelation. The entire Old Testament phrase is something like: *"blue, purple, scarlet and fine twisted linen."* But, here in Revelation we have a notable lack of the color blue. We will talk about this omission in detail later.

An example of its usage is in Exodus 26:1:

> *"Moreover thou shalt make the tabernacle with ten curtains of **fine twined linen, and blue, and purple, and scarlet**: with cherubims of cunning work shalt thou make them."*

These curtains of the temple were by no means the only things that were supposed to consist of blue, purple, scarlet, and fine linen. The same phrase was used in relation to the following items:

1. The curtains of the tabernacle

2. The veil of the temple

3. The hanging for the door of the tent with lampstands

4. The hanging for the gate of the court

5. Certain offerings

6. Cloths of service

7. The girdle of the high priest

8. The ephod of the high priest

9. The breastplate of the high priest

10. The stitched pomegranates on the high priest's garments

Almost everything in the service of the temple that was made from cloth was to be made out of these colors.

As we progress, what will be of particular interest to us is the relationship between the clothes of Mystery Babylon and the clothes of the high priest.

Notice, though, there is a difference between what was said of the clothing of Mystery Babylon ("…and the woman was arrayed in purple and scarlet colour…") and the clothing of the high priest and the various items associated with temple worship ("**...blue**, purple, scarlet and **fine twined linen...**)."

At first, it would seem that fine linen is not mentioned in relationship to Mystery Babylon either, but in a later verse (Rev 18:16) it actually does mention "fine linen" as well.

> *"And saying, 'Alas, alas, that great city, **that was clothed in fine linen**, and purple, and scarlet, and decked with gold, and precious stones, and pearls!' – Rev 18:16*

So the main difference between the clothing of Mystery Babylon and the clothing of the high priest is the color blue. This could be due to the significance that the Bible put on the color blue in relation to its symbolism of being in a right standing with God and His commandments as well as it being a symbol of their not "whoring" any more:

> *"Speak unto the children of Israel, and bid them that they make them fringes in the borders of their garments throughout their generations, and that they put upon the fringe of the borders **a ribband of blue:** And it shall be unto you for a fringe, that ye may **look upon it, and remember all the commandments of the LORD, and do them**; and that ye seek not after your own heart and your own eyes, after which ye use to go a **whoring:** That ye may **remember, and do all my commandments, and be holy unto your God.**" - Num 15:38-40*

The Ark of the Covenant in the Tabernacle was also covered with blue cloth (Numbers 4:5-7; 11-13), and the robe of the High Priest was also blue.

I am suggesting that she is wearing the clothing of a harlot high priest who is promoting the worship, not of the true God in temple service, but of the antichrist, who also will make use of the temple.

This interpretation is greatly strengthened when we get to the next verse, which is about the name on the woman's forehead. We will see the connection to the high priest and the name that was on his forehead. But for now let's continue on with the present verse.

"...decked with gold and precious stones and pearls"

Decked is really the key word here. It is a different Greek word than the word "**arrayed**" earlier in the verse. The word "decked" has to do with jewels. One definition says that it means: "to bring an ornament upon." Decked is not a very common word in the Old Testament. In fact, it is only used 10 times, and it has very provocative uses.

The overall picture of its use in the Old Testament is God saying that He decked Jerusalem with precious jewels when she was in her youth; but as she began to commit adultery by the worship of pagan gods, she then begins to "deck" herself in a different manner.

For example, here in the first part of Ezekiel 16, we see how God decked her in her proverbial youth:

> "'*I decked thee also with ornaments*, *and I put bracelets upon thy hands, and a chain on thy neck. And I put a jewel on thy forehead, and earrings in thine ears, and a beautiful crown upon thine head. Thus wast thou decked with gold and silver; and thy raiment was of fine linen, and silk, and broidered work; thou didst eat fine flour, and honey, and oil: and thou wast exceeding beautiful, and thou didst prosper into a kingdom. And thy renown went forth among the heathen for thy beauty: for it was perfect through my comeliness, which I had put upon thee', saith the Lord GOD. 'But thou didst trust in thine own beauty, and playedst the harlot because of thy renown, and pouredst out thy fornications on every one that passed by; his it was.'" - Eze 16:11-15*

Then later, when Jerusalem becomes a prostitute, she decks herself a different way:

> "*And furthermore, that ye have sent for men to come from far, unto whom a messenger was sent; and, lo, they came: for whom thou didst wash thyself, paintedst thy eyes, and **deckedst thyself with ornaments**." - Eze 23:40*

And in Hosea 2:13:

> "'*And I will visit upon her the days of Baalim, wherein she burned*

*incense to them, and she **decked herself with her earrings and her
jewels, and she went after her lovers, and forgat me**,' saith the
LORD." – Hos 2:13*

But one of the most provocative uses of the word "decked" in relation to our
verse in Revelation 17:4 is found in Jeremiah 4:29-30 while speaking of the
city of Jerusalem. It says:

> *"Though thou clothest thyself with crimson, though **thou deckest
> thee with ornaments of gold**, though thou rentest thy face with
> painting, in vain shalt thou make thyself fair; **thy lovers will despise
> thee, they will seek thy life."** – Jer 4:30*

The connections to Mystery Babylon here should be quite obvious. It is also
interesting to note that in this passage Jerusalem's lover was prophesied to
despise her and take her life. This is exactly what the beast which she calls
her husband does; he turns on her and attacks the city.

One interesting thing in this verse is the mention of **pearls**. I found this
reference somewhat curious, as there is only one mention of pearls in the OT.
In fact, there are only eight references in the entire Bible, and half of those
are in the book of Revelation. Three of the other references are using pearls
as an example of something valuable, like "the pearl of great price" or "don't
throw your pearls before swine." The only pearl reference left is also one that
I think is applicable to this verse. It is found in 1 Timothy 2:9:

> *"In like manner also, that women adorn themselves in modest
> apparel, with shamefacedness and sobriety; not with broided hair,
> or gold, or **pearls**, or costly array..." – 1Tim 2:9*

Here, being decked with pearls is used as the opposite of modest clothing.
That would seem to fit the description of Mystery Babylon, but there may be
yet more significance to it that I am not aware of.

"having a golden cup in her hand full of abominations and filthiness of her fornication..."

The only other time this phrase "golden cup" appears in the Bible that I know
of is in Jer. 51:7. I'm sure it is not a coincidence that the entire chapter of

Jeremiah 51 is talking about the actual fall of Babylon the city, which I believe is a prefiguration of Mystery Babylon's fall.

Many parallels can be seen between these two chapters if you read them carefully. This phrase **golden cup** is certainly one of them. The verse reads:

> *"Babylon hath been a **golden cup** in the LORD'S hand, that made all the earth drunken: the nations have drunken of her wine; therefore the nations are mad." – Jer 51:7*

Also notice here that the nations are drunk with the wine in the cup. It makes them "mad." This is a direct parallel to Revelation 17:2 which says:

> *"With whom the kings of the earth have committed fornication, and the inhabitants of the earth have been made drunk with the wine **of her** fornication." – Rev 17:2*

This is often missed, but I think very important - what is in the cup is **her** own sin, **her** own idolatry, and the nations are made drunk by it.

I think that Revelation 18:3 gives us more detail on this:

> *"For all nations have drunk of the wine of the **wrath of her fornication**, and the kings of the earth have committed fornication with her, and the merchants of the earth are waxed rich through the abundance of her delicacies." - Rev 18:3*

This phrase: "wine of the wrath of her fornication," as the KJV has it, is kind of an odd way to put it in my opinion. I think the ESV captures the sense of this verse when it says:

> *"For all nations have drunk the wine of the **passion** of her [fornication]..."*

What I'm suggesting here is that she is so passionately promoting the antichrist as her messiah, as her god, that it entices the world to join her in her fornication, and they then also commit this abomination themselves. It is largely because of her own fierce promotion of this idolatry that the world joins her in this sin of worship of the antichrist. It is also in this sense that she fulfills the role of an idolatrous high priest.

Rev 18:4 expands on this idea that **her** own sin is causing others to sin:

> *"And I heard another voice from heaven, saying, 'Come out of her, my people, that ye be not partakers of **her sins**, and that ye receive not of her plagues.'"* – Rev 18:4

(Rev 17:5)

And upon her forehead was a name written, 'MYSTERY, BABYLON THE GREAT, THE MOTHER OF HARLOTS AND ABOMINATIONS OF THE EARTH.

The first thing I want to focus in on is this phrase **"upon her forehead."**

There are two notable things about foreheads in the Old Testament that are going to be important. The first is in relation to the high priest's uniform. In Exodus 28, it is discussing the headband of the high priest, and says:

> *"And thou shalt make a plate of pure gold, and grave upon it, like the engravings of a signet, **HOLINESS TO THE LORD**. And thou shalt put it on a blue lace, that it may be upon the mitre; upon the forefront of the mitre it shall be. And it shall be upon **Aaron's forehead**, that Aaron may bear the iniquity of the holy things, which the children of Israel shall hallow in all their holy gifts; and it shall be **always upon his forehead**, that they may be accepted before the LORD."* – Exo 28:36-38

This is a very interesting bit of information considering the connection to the high priest's garments we have already seen. The High Priest had a gold plate that covered his forehead with the words "HOLINESS TO THE LORD" engraved on it.

This is compared with Mystery Babylon, the harlot high priest, who has on her forehead the following words:

"MYSTERY, BABYLON THE GREAT, THE MOTHER OF HARLOTS "

This brings us to the other usage of foreheads in the OT, which I think is also at play here:

> *"Therefore the showers have been withholden, and there hath been no latter rain; and thou hadst **a whore's forehead**, thou refusedst to be ashamed." – Jer 3:3*

There is a refusal to be ashamed of her idolatry here, which is exemplified in Mystery Babylon by the proud boasting of her abominations, which are written on her forehead.

I don't think this should be understood as her knowing that she is worshiping and promoting the antichrist, because she does say that she is not a "widow" and that she sits as a "queen." I think it just means that her promotion of the antichrist as Messiah will be very bold and out in the open, as the verse of the ESV said: "the passion of her [fornication]" is what will intoxicate the masses.

"MYSTERY,"

Notice the comma in the King James, as in "**Mystery, Babylon.**" The name is not a proper name **Mystery Babylon**, as I have been using it, and probably will continue to use it, but rather the "Mystery" here is signifying that there is something secret about the name "Babylon the Great." Other translations reflect this better in my opinion, for instance:

> *(The Geneva Bible) "And in her forehead was a name written, **A mysterie**, that great Babylon, that mother of whoredomes, and abominations of the earth...."*

> *(ESV) "And on her forehead **was written a name of mystery**: "Babylon the great, mother of prostitutes and of earth's abominations."*

> *(ISV-v2.0) "On her forehead **was written a secret name**: BABYLON THE GREAT, THE MOTHER OF PROSTITUTES AND DETESTABLE THINGS OF THE EARTH."*

The word in Greek for **Mystery** is: *mustrion*. It means: a *secret* or "Mystery," though there is an idea of *silence* imposed by *initiation* into religious rites as well; in other words it's a secret that can be discovered without it being revealed to you.

The simple fact that the name Babylon is a "mystery" is a strong argument *against* MB being the literal city Babylon.

This idea of giving cities spiritual names, depending on the type of characteristics they exhibit or have exhibited, is demonstrated earlier in the book of Revelation when it calls Jerusalem by two "spiritual" names. It says, speaking of the two witnesses:

> *"And their dead bodies will lie in the street of the great city* **which spiritually is called Sodom and Egypt,** *where also our Lord was crucified." – Rev 11:8*

Later on we will look more in depth at this verse, but now I only want to call your attention to some of the other spiritual names given to Jerusalem here: Sodom and Egypt. Both are cities known inter- biblically for their various sins, and when Jerusalem acts like one of these notorious cities, the Bible calls it by those names instead of its actual name.

On this phrase, **"THE GREAT,"** the Bible commentator Adam Clark said:

> *"This woman is also called Babylon* **the Great**; *she is the exact antitype of the ancient Babylon in her idolatry and cruelty, but the ancient city called Babylon* **is only a drawing of her in miniature.** *This is indeed Babylon The Great." - Clark[3]*

"...MOTHER OF HARLOTS..."

We have already discussed the lack of the word all here, as in the "mother of **all** harlots." Some try to make this phrase more than the text makes of it. This city is the mother of harlots, she is the harlot of harlots; she is the mother of harlots - in the sense that she is the worst one of all.

A consistent idiom in Scripture is that cites have children, which are often referred to as daughters or simply children of that city.

One example was with Jesus, when on the road to be crucified said this:

> *"But Jesus turning unto them said, **Daughters of Jerusalem**, weep not for me, but weep for yourselves, and for your children. For, behold, the days are coming, in which they shall say, 'Blessed are the barren, and the wombs that never bare, and the paps which never gave suck.'"- Luk 23:28-29*

In Isaiah 4:4, when speaking of the institution of the millennial kingdom it says this:

> *"When the Lord has washed away the filth of the **daughters of Zion**, and purged the blood of Jerusalem from her midst, by the spirit of judgment and by the spirit of burning." – Isa 4:4*

A side note here is that this purging of Jerusalem in the context of Isaiah 4 happens just before the millennial reign, exactly the place that Mystery Babylon is judged in Rev 16-19. This is strong support for a double fulfillment of the judgments of Jerusalem.

Yet another example of the inhabitants of a city being referred to as children of that city is:

> *"O Jerusalem, Jerusalem, the one who kills the prophets and stones those who are sent to her! How often I wanted to gather **your children** together, as a hen gathers her chicks under her wings, but you were not willing! See! Your house is left to you desolate..." – Mat 23:37-38*

"...ABOMINATIONS OF THE EARTH...."

More parallels to Jerusalem are seen here in Jeremiah 6 where it says:

> *"'Were they [the people of Jerusalem] ashamed when they had committed **abomination**? No! They were not at all ashamed; Nor did they know how to blush. Therefore they shall fall among those who fall; At the time I punish them, They shall be cast down, says the*

LORD." – Jer 6:15

The word **"Abominations"** is used pretty consistently in Scripture as that which is absolutely detestable to the LORD, but especially that of grievous idolatry and false worship. The "abomination of desolation" spoken of by Daniel, Jesus and Paul is of note here when the antichrist declares himself to be God in the temple. This would be the ultimate abomination, one that will ultimately involve the entire world.

(Rev 17:6)

And I saw the woman drunken with the blood of the saints, and with the blood of the martyrs of Jesus: and when I saw her, I wondered with great admiration.

This verse is one that is often used to prove that the woman is Rome, Islam, or even an allegorical pagan system from time immemorial.

This verse is simply talking about persecution. The "woman" here kills a lot of saints. The commentators always try to prove that *their* version of Mystery Babylon has killed more than the other candidates for Mystery Babylon. I suppose whoever quotes the highest number of saints killed wins, accurate or not.

I suppose I will also join in this game, but unlike them, I have explicit biblical support that the worst persecution of all time will come out of, and have its epicenter in, Jerusalem.

Speaking of the "Abomination of Desolation" which will occur at the temple mount in Jerusalem, Jesus says in Matthew 24:

> *"When ye therefore shall see the abomination of desolation, spoken of by Daniel the prophet, stand in the holy place, (whoso readeth, let him understand:) Then let them which be in **Judaea** flee into the mountains: Let him which is on the housetop not come down to take any thing out of his house: Neither let him which is in the field return back to take his clothes. And woe unto them that are with*

*child, and to them that give suck in those days! But pray ye that your flight be not in the winter, neither on the sabbath day: For then shall be great tribulation, **such as was not since the beginning of the world to this time, no, nor ever shall be.** And except those days should be shortened, **there should no flesh be saved**: but for the **elect's sake** those days shall be shortened." - Mat 24:15-22*

So this killing will be so bad that if its days were not cut short, then none of the elect would even survive! Jesus also says that this will be more severe than **any before it** or **any after it**. The worst religious genocide of all time, and its epicenter is the city of Jerusalem.

The very fact that the Lord is emphasizing the importance of fleeing quickly when they see the abomination of desolation is proof that there will be many in Jerusalem that will not consider the antichrist's seating himself in the temple and declaring himself to be God an abomination at all! In fact, just the opposite, they apparently begin to carry out the antichrist's orders to kill Christians at this point. This killing may indeed spread to the entire world from here, but the fact that its epicenter is the city of Jerusalem is one of the most attested to prophetic events in the Bible.

"blood of the saints, and with the blood of the martyrs of Jesus:"

Saints and Martyrs could be referring to those killed after the abomination of desolation.

Jesus said that the people killed by the antichrist will be killed because of His "names' sake" (Mat 24:9).

We know that in addition to **Saints and Martyrs**, "prophets" are twice added to this list of those that MB kills:

*"And in her was found the blood of **prophets**, and of saints…"* – Rev 18:24a

It is also notable that the two witnesses, who are called "prophets" in Rev 11:10, are said to be killed in the city of Jerusalem:

"And their dead bodies shall lie in the street of the great city, which

spiritually is called Sodom and Egypt, **where also our Lord was crucified.** *" – Rev 11:8*

The city "where our Lord was crucified" is unambiguously Jerusalem.

The Angel's Interpretation

(Rev 17:7)

And the angel said unto me, 'Wherefore didst thou marvel? I will tell thee the mystery of the woman, and of the beast that carrieth her, which hath the seven heads and ten horns.

"...And the angel said unto me..."

The angel is going to tell John what it is he has been seeing so far. There are many examples in Scripture of a prophet seeing a vision that they did not fully understand until an angel interpreted it for them. We find examples of this in Daniel, Zechariah, and several times in the book of Revelation.

"...I will tell thee the mystery of the woman, and of the beast that carrieth her, which hath the seven heads and ten horns.'"

It is so important to keep in mind that there are two distinct characters in this vision: the woman, known as Mystery Babylon, and the seven-headed, ten-horned beast, which she rides.

Mystery Babylon, which the angel will later say is a city, is riding the seven-headed, ten-horned beast, which is the antichrist. This seven-headed, ten-horned beast will later turn on her and kill her (Rev 17:12-16). I emphasize that these two are distinct because some folks, when studying these passages, forget this distinction, and failing to see it can cause an incorrect understanding of this prophecy.

(Rev 17:8)

The beast that thou sawest was, and is not; and shall ascend out of the bottomless pit, and go into perdition: and they that dwell on the earth

31

shall wonder, whose names were not written in the book of life from the foundation of the world, when they behold the beast that was, and is not, and yet is.

So the angel begins to talk to John about the seven-headed, ten-horned beast that it mentioned in the previous verse.

Let's also go back to the beginning of this particular vision in Rev 17 so we can see the full description John gives to this seven-headed, ten-horned beast:

> *"...scarlet coloured beast, full of names of blasphemy, having seven heads and ten horns." – Rev 17:3b*

Here we also pick up the additional information that this seven-headed, ten-horned beast was also scarlet and was "full of names of blasphemy."

This is the same description given to the beast four chapters earlier in Revelation chapter 13, which is about the antichrist. The beast in that chapter also has seven heads, ten horns and has "names of blasphemy." This is not coincidental, nor is it the only time in our verse, Revelation 17:8, that there is an explicit reference to Revelation 13 about the antichrist beast.

In fact, I intend to show that the angel gives almost no new information in this verse. The new information from the angel about this beast will come after this verse, but verse 8 here almost serves as a very long re-introduction to the antichrist beast of Revelation 13, using titles and descriptions of him already clearly established.

For example, consider the part of this verse that says **"they that dwell on the earth,"** or the earth dwellers, which is kind of a technical term for those that are unsaved, as it clarifies here by adding that **"their names are not written in the book of life."** These earth dwellers will worship the beast that "was and is not and yet is."

This was not new information to John in Revelation 17 because he wrote the same description of the beast in Revelation 13 using identical language.

> *"And all that **dwell upon the earth shall worship him, whose names are not written in the book of life** of the Lamb slain from the*

foundation of the world." – Rev 13:8

The angel back in our verse is calling to remembrance the beast that John has already seen with these exact phrases and descriptions. We will see that even the little things are important – for example the earth dwellers **"wondering"** in this verse is a reference to their "wondering" at the beast in chapter 13.

"Was, and is not; and shall ascend out of the bottomless pit, and go into perdition..."

This phrase gives people a great deal of difficulty, and so we will spend a bit of time on it. I intend to show that this idea of "was, and is not, and coming out of the bottomless pit" is a title referring to the antichrist having been miraculously healed, or resurrected from the dead.

The last phrase in this verse, **"...the beast that was, and is not, and yet is..."** being another way to say the same thing – that is he lives, he dies, and he seems to rise again, and will ultimately go to destruction or perdition. It's sort of a chronology of his entire career on earth, and it functions as a title on several occasions in the book of Revelation.

Before I begin to explain the details of this, we need to refresh our memories to the significance that the Bible puts on the seeming resurrection of the antichrist from the dead.

Let's review Revelation 13, which is primarily about the antichrist, to make sure we understand this preliminary idea. In the relatively short chapter of Revelation 13, it mentions the antichrist's fatal wound that was healed three times. The first instance is in verse 3:

> *"And I saw one of his heads as it were **wounded to death; and his deadly wound was healed: and all the world wondered after the beast**. And they worshiped the dragon, which gave power unto the beast: and they worshiped the beast, saying, 'Who is like unto the beast? Who is able to make war with him?'" – Rev 13:3-4*

Here it seems to imply that the world's worship of the beast is directly connected to his deadly wound being healed. It says that they "wondered after him saying "Who can make war with him?" This is the exact same word used in or current verse: "**wondered**." It is also in the exact same context, i.e., wonder from the earth dwellers, associated with worship, and the antichrist's apparent resurrection from the dead.

This is one of the first descriptions of the antichrist we are given in Revelation 13, right after the symbolic imagery of verses 1 and 2. This is the first thing that we are told about the beast – that he has a deadly wound that is healed. The Bible, as we will see, considers this event <u>very important</u>.

By the second reference to this event in verse 12, the idea of a healed deadly wound has become a title or an identifying description of the beast. Here it distinguishes the first beast from the second by adding the clarification: "**whose deadly wound was healed**."

> *"And he [false prophet] exerciseth all the power of the first beast [antichrist] before him, and causeth the earth and them which dwell therein to worship the first beast, **whose deadly wound was healed**." – Rev: 13:12*

And in the third reference in Rev: 13:14, we see that the healed deadly wound is used again as a title or distinguishing characteristic of the antichrist beast. Here it says:

> *"And [the false prophet] deceiveth them that dwell on the earth by the means of those miracles which he had power to do in the sight of the beast; saying to them that dwell on the earth, that they should make an image to the beast, **which had the wound by a sword, and did live**." - Rev 13:14*

So we see again this idea of a resurrection being used as a type of title and to distinguish which beast is in view. Therefore, this phrase "**was, and is not; and shall ascend out of the bottomless pit**" is basically just another way of saying the same thing. It is an identifier as to which beast we are talking about, the one that **was** (lived), **is not** (died), **and shall ascend out of the bottomless pit** (come back from the dead).

Arthur Pink, an early English Bible scholar who wrote extensively on the antichrist, agrees. He said the following:
> *"A further reference to the resurrection of the Antichrist, his coming*

forth from the Bottomless Pit, is found in Rev. 17:8.... It is to be noted that the earth-dwellers wonder when they behold the Beast that was (alive), and is not (now alive), and yet is (raised again). The world will then be presented with the spectacle of a man raised from the dead." – Pink[4]

Pink, as well as many other people, associate the phrase "**coming out of the bottomless pit**" in Revelation 17:8 with the apparent resurrection of the antichrist in Revelation 13. We will see explicit biblical proof of this interpretation in just a moment.

The Bible uses the word "abyss," which is here translated as "bottomless pit" in many different ways: it is a prison for spirits in Mark 5 and it is almost synonymous with the abode of the dead.

This word, "abyss," is also the same word that the apostle Paul uses to describe where Jesus went during at least part of the three days in which He was dead before He resurrected.

> *"But the righteousness which is of faith speaketh on this wise, 'Say not in thine heart, "Who shall ascend into heaven? (that is, to bring Christ down from above:) Or, "Who shall descend into the **deep**? [abyss] (that is, to bring up Christ again from the dead.)" - Rom 10:6-7*

So this same word for "bottomless pit" or "abyss" <u>is also the place where Christ came out of when He resurrected.</u>

We find more detail on this event in Acts 2:27-32 where Peter starts off by quoting from the Old Testament:

> *"**Because thou wilt not leave my soul in hell [hades]**, neither wilt thou suffer thine Holy One to see corruption. Thou hast made known to me the ways of life; thou shalt make me full of joy with thy countenance. Men and brethren, let me freely speak unto you of the patriarch, David – that he is both dead and buried, and his sepulchre is with us unto this day. Therefore being a prophet, and knowing that God had sworn with an oath to him, that of the fruit of his loins, according to the flesh, he would raise up Christ to sit on*

his throne; He seeing this before spake of the resurrection of Christ,
that his soul was not left in hell [hades], *neither his flesh did see*
corruption. This Jesus hath God raised up, whereof we all are
witnesses. - Act 2:27-32

Now this is interesting because the word "hades" here was mentioned by
Peter as the place where Jesus' soul went when He died, when Paul says that
it was the abyss. But we can see that contextually they are both talking about
the place where Jesus' soul went during His death.

My point is not to do an exhaustive study on this subject, but only to show
that Jesus went to the abyss at some point during His death. He may have also
gone to other locations in hades such as paradise and even "Tatarus."

There are more references to this event which I will leave for you to study
further:

Eph. 4:8-10, 1 Pet. 3:18-20, 2 Pet. 2:4-5, Mat. 12:38-45 and Luke 23:43.

My only point is that coming up from the "abyss" can be shown from
Scripture to mean <u>resurrection from the dead</u>.

So these phrases are used like a title referring to the antichrist's apparent
resurrection from the dead. It is as if it is a chronology of his career and a title
all at the same time. He is the beast that lives, dies, resurrects, and ultimately
meets his doom in perdition or the lake of fire in Revelation 19:20.

I would suggest that the following phrases are all referring not only to the
same person – the antichrist, but also the same identifying event in that
person's life – his apparent resurrection.

1. The beast that was, and is not, and yet is

2. The beast that was, and is not; and shall ascend out of the
    bottomless pit, and go into perdition

3. The first beast, whose deadly wound was healed.

4. The beast, which had the wound by a sword, and did live

5.   The beast that ascendeth out of the bottomless pit

So back in Revelation 17:8, the angel is about to explain some very interesting details to John about the seven-headed beast that John saw, but this entire verse is basically preliminary. It is simply the restating of the characteristics of the beast of Revelation 13, to clarify that the beast he saw is the same one he saw in a previous vision.

But before we get to new information about the beast, there is one more aspect of this verse that must be covered. There are a lot of interpretations that, even while understanding that the phrases like **"the beast that was and is not and yet is..."** are referring to the antichrist's resurrection, which will say that the tense of some of the words in these verses makes it necessary for the antichrist to have lived before the time of John. They will say that since John wrote in the late 1st century, the past tense of the word **"was"** in the first part of the phrase, i.e., **"the beast that was,"** means that the beast that will come to life in the future as antichrist must have lived some time before the time of John.

Common candidates for the antichrist proposed in this scenario are Hitler, Judas, or even Nimrod. Again, they are saying that the beast that is "yet to come" must have been dead already when John was writing. This view can lead to any number of wrong conclusions about the identity of the antichrist in my opinion.

They fail to see that John consistently uses these phrases like **"the beast that was, and is not, and yet is,"** as a title for the beast of his visions – visions in which he sees all the way to the end of knowable time in some cases. Yet he never ceases to refer to everything he sees *as having happened in the past*. For instance, even the New Jerusalem's descent in Revelation 21, which is almost universally considered to be a future event, must have already descended in the first century if this was the correct way to view the text. Because John said, "And I John **saw** [past tense] the holy city, new Jerusalem, coming down...".

More to this specific point about the phrases like **"was and is not and yet is,"** if you applied it consistently to the other titles that refer to the antichrist's resurrection, the theory that the beast must have already existed like Judas or

Nimrod would quickly break down.

1. The beast that was, and is not, and yet is

2. The beast that was, and is not; and shall ascend out of the bottomless pit, and go into perdition

3. The first beast, **whose deadly wound was healed**

4. The beast, which had **the wound by a sword, and did live**

5. The beast that ascendeth out of the bottomless pit

So if we applied this 1st century tense idea to these other passages, we must also conclude that the antichrist not only has lived and died by the time of John, but also that his wound had to have already been healed in the 1st century as well because John also refers to it in the past tense!

This would, of course, not be agreed upon by those making this claim. They would not say that this pre- John character has risen from the dead yet; they would only say that he would have already died before John's time.

The answer here is to realize that phrases like "**the beast that was, and is not, and yet is**," "**The beast, which had the wound by a sword, and did live**," or "**The first beast, whose deadly wound was healed**" have the same function as being a way to refer to the antichrist. They can even be used to refer to the defining event of his life and also the entire end times course of events. The tense being used is the exact tense you would expect from someone who was trying to refer back to an event he saw in a vision that consisted of future events. In theology it is called the "Prophetic perfect tense."[5]

It is also notable that the words in the phrase are in the exact order one would expect to see if this was true. For instance, "coming out of the abyss" would seem to be the first thing mentioned in this phrase if it was in fact referring to where he initially comes from; but instead we see it being consistently placed precisely after he was "**not**" or after he dies, exactly where you would expect to see a reference to his resurrection.

I will show what I believe to be proof of this when we get to verse 11.

(Rev 17:9-10)

And here is the mind which hath wisdom. The seven heads are seven mountains, on which the woman sitteth. And there are seven kings: five are fallen, and one is, and the other is not yet come; and when he cometh, he must continue a short space.

This is when the angel begins to tell us more about the seven-headed, ten-horned beast.

"Here *is* the mind which hath wisdom..."

It says the same thing earlier when it is talking about the mark of the beast:

> *"**Here is wisdom**. Let him that hath understanding count the number of the beast: for it is the number of a man; and his number is Six hundred threescore and six." – Rev 13:18*

I think it may have something to do with how the next idea should be viewed.

"The seven heads are seven mountains, on which the woman sitteth. And there are seven kings..."

Now we come to one of the most misunderstood passages in this chapter. You know how I said I have found ninety-plus characteristics of Mystery Babylon so far? Well, most commentators seem to think there is only one, and that is that the city of Mystery Babylon sits on "seven hills," which they derive from their interpretation of this verse. Often they will say that this city on seven hills is Rome, which is famous for its seven hills, but it doesn't stop those who think Mystery Babylon is Mecca or even Jerusalem from claiming that their city also sits on seven hills. The only problem is that this is not what this verse is talking about at all.

There are many ways to show this is true, grammatically, contextually, logically, and by comparing Scripture with other Scripture.

Let's start with the grammar.

Revelation 17:9-10

(KJV) And here *is* the mind which hath wisdom. The seven heads are seven mountains, on which the woman sitteth. **And there are seven kings:** five are fallen, and one is, *and* the other is not yet come; and when he cometh, he must continue a short space.

(ESV) This calls for a mind with wisdom: the seven heads are seven mountains on which the woman is seated; **they are also seven kings**, five of whom have fallen, one is, the other has not yet come, and when he does come he must remain only a little while.

The key is in this phrase: "**...And there are seven kings.**" This is how it reads in the KJV, which I have been doing this study in. Other versions render this with a very important distinction. They say that the seven heads of the beast are seven mountains; the angel then further defines these mountains as being seven kings.

Such as the ESV which says:

(ESV) "**...they are also seven kings**, five of whom have fallen, one is, the other has not yet come..."

You can see the difference. The King James gives us the idea that the angel begins to talk about a totally separate thing when it talks about the kings, whereas the ESV defines the seven mountains as seven kings and then begins to give further info about these kings. Well...which one is right?

You should know that this difference in translation is not an issue with the

Greek texts, like the Textus Receptus or the Wescott and Hort. The Greek texts say the exact same thing here, so it's not one of those issues. This is simply a matter of translator error.

Revelation 17:9-10

(ASV) and they are seven kings
(ESV) they are also seven kings,
(NIV) They are also seven kings.
(NASB) and they are seven kings
(HSB) They are also seven kings:
(RSV) they are also seven kings
(Geneva) They are also seuen King
(ERV) and they are seven kings
(NAB) and they are seven kings

There is near universal agreement among Bible translators that the grammar is saying that the seven mountains are in fact seven kings. Here we see this is the way it is translated in almost every major English Bible.

Grammatically, a major reason for this is that the word εἰσιν [eisin] here translated as "there are" is the 3rd-person plural of εἰμι [eimi], meaning *I am*, which should be rendered *they are*.

When describing the ten horns a few verses later, a similar phrase occurs: [deka basileis eisin]. There, the KJV and NKJV translate the phrase correctly, without substituting *there* for *they* as is done in verse 10.

Revelation 17:9-10

And here *is* the mind which hath wisdom. The seven heads are **seven mountains**, on which the woman sitteth. And there are εἰσιν [eisin] **seven kings:** five are fallen, and one is, *and* the other is not yet come; and when he cometh, he must continue a short space. - Rev 17:9-10 (KJV)

And **the ten horns** which thou sawest are **ten kings**, - Rev 17:12a

I am not a Greek scholar and I would not want anyone to believe me based on my explaining this to you grammatically, so let's move to showing that the angel is telling us that the seven heads are seven kings by the context of the passage and by comparing Scripture with other Scripture.

I want to start by reiterating that all the other times in chapter 17 that the seven-headed beast with ten horns is mentioned, it seems to go out of its way to use phrases that are used back in Revelation 13.

And we saw that the beast in our chapter (17) has many of the same characteristics as the one we looked at in Revelation 13. They both had seven heads, ten horns, they both had names of blasphemy on their heads, they both were referred to by their having been killed yet living, they both have the earth dwellers wonder at them when they see their apparent resurrection, and they both have people whose names were not written in the book of life worship them. I know this seems almost obvious, but you should know that the view that the seven mountains are seven hills of a city prevents people from seeing this most basic point.

Our passage goes on to say that one of these heads, which are kings, is the same "was and is not" king talked about in Revelation 13 who gets the mortal wound. Let's flip back to Revelation 13:3 and check it out:

"One of its heads seemed to have a mortal wound, but its mortal wound was healed, and the whole earth marveled as they followed the beast." – Rev 13:3

So you see here that one of the beast's seven heads is referred to as having a mortal wound. This is an exact match with our verse if you are willing to admit that Revelation 17:9 has nothing to do with physical hills in Rome, Mecca, Jerusalem or anywhere else. I mean, do you really think that one of the hills in Rome is going to be mortally wounded and then come back to life? Or that everyone marvels at and begins to worship a hill?

"Five of whom have fallen, one is, the other has not yet come…"

This will explain how this seven-headed beast and its heads work. The question I always had was this: if the seven-headed, ten-horned beast was supposed to be the antichrist, how come only one of the heads of this antichrist appears to be in view?

The Bible unapologetically disregards the other 6 heads of this beast as basically unimportant and really only tells us about one of these heads; and somehow both the entire beast and this one specific head are called the antichrist.

Well, this verse will explain that issue.

"Five of whom have fallen, one is, the other has not yet come…"

It says five of these kings have fallen. **Fallen**, among other things, is a biblical term for having died (Exodus 32:28, I Samuel 4:10, 2 Samuel 1:19, 1 Chronicles 5:10). **"One is,"** presumably means one was currently living in John's day, and **"one is yet to come."**

The beast, as the spirit of the antichrist, has manifested itself in the form of particularly antichrist-like kings throughout history. In 1 John 2:18 it says the following:

"Children, it is the last hour, and as you have heard that antichrist

*is coming, **so now many antichrists have come.** Therefore we know that it is the last hour. —1Jn 2:18*

I believe these five fallen antichrist kings can be determined using no other tool than the Bible: These would be kings that are biblically obvious types of the antichrist. For example **Pharaoh** during the time of the Exodus is probably one of them, **Antiochus Epiphanes** who Daniel spent so much time describing, is clearly a type of antichrist, with his setting himself in the temple and declaring himself to be god. Sennacherib, the King of Tyre, Nimrod, and Nero have all been proposed as types of antichrist in the past.

I am not going to attempt to give you a perfect list of these five fallen kings, but I will say that I think they can be determined using the Bible alone.

Some people would say that these heads are not physical kings at all but rather kingdoms. They do this by adding a step to the angel's interpretation of the seven heads of the beast. The angel says the seven heads are seven mountains, which are seven kings, but they will add a step to this and say the seven kings are seven kingdoms.

They rationalize this by pointing out that in the book of Daniel, kings and kingdoms are pretty much interchangeable terms. Often, before they will take you to this verse in Revelation 17, they will have you agree to the condition that kings mean kingdoms. If you agree, then they will have you flip to Revelation 17 and say, "Well then, we know that these kings are not kings, but actually seven kingdoms."

I don't believe this is a good way to interpret the Bible, especially because John is a different writer than Daniel, and he uses the word king several times to refer to an obvious individual king. In Rev 10:11, he even seems to contrast the kings with kingdoms or nations:

> *"And he said unto me, 'Thou must prophesy again before many peoples, and nations, and tongues, and kings." – Rev. 10:11*

But I think the obvious thing is that the antichrist in Daniel, Matthew 24 and parallel passages, 2 Thessalonians and Revelation is always referred to as a man. He does things that only a man can do. He sits in a temple in Jerusalem and declares himself to be god. He is called a man on several occasions. It says he won't regard the "God of his fathers." I could go on, but my point is that it takes twice as much work to make the antichrist be a kingdom rather than a king.

I would say that the antichrist will be a part of and control specific kingdoms, which is important to the book of Daniel and Revelation, but the fact that there is a man that moves and rules those kingdoms is attested to over and over again in Scripture.

"One is…"

I will not speculate as to which king was the manifestation of the antichrist in John's day either, as I honestly don't know myself. Some speculate Nero, but I have not decided what my view is on this point.

"The other has not yet come…"

This is one that I think we can have more explicit biblical information about.

So this future king, this future manifestation of the beast, has at least one specific characteristic mentioned here. He **"must continue a short space."**

I believe this phrase is strong evidence that the king that is future, is the one that has the fatal wound and yet lives, the antichrist head. The head we have been discussing in Revelation 13 – the one that so much time is spent on.

This idea of a **"short space"** is good evidence to that effect.

By far, the most talked about time period in prophecy is the 3.5 years which the antichrist is given. It makes reference to this exact time period seven times in Scripture and talks about the detail of it in many more places. It refers to this 3.5-year period in the following ways:

1.   42 months

2.   1260 days

3.   A time, times, and half a time

It refers to this time period being a **"short time"** as well; in fact, using the exact words from Rev 17:10 when it says:

> *"Therefore rejoice, ye heavens, and ye that dwell in them. Woe to the inhabiters of the earth and of the sea! for the devil is come down unto you, having great wrath, because he knoweth that he hath but a* **short time.** *" – Rev 12:12*

The idea that he must continue a short time seems to match up well with the references about the antichrist who has the mortal wound and lives. It says in Revelation 13:5:

> *"And there was given unto him a mouth speaking great things and blasphemies; and* **power was given unto him to continue forty and two months.** *" - Rev 13:5*

Rarely are characteristics of the antichrist found in only one verse. This idea is backed up in several places:

> *"And he shall speak great words against the most High, and shall wear out the saints of the most High, and think to change times and laws: and they shall be given into his hand* **until a time and times and the dividing of time.** *" – Dan 7:25*

I would propose that this idea of **"short space"** is referring back to the short space given for the dragon to continue in Revelation 12 and the 3.5-year period given to the antichrist in Revelation 13. It also should be noted that 3.5 years is an extremely short time for a king to rule.

Other people who want to make this future king one that has already been alive in the past, like Nimrod, will propose that the yet to come king of Rev 17:10 was Hitler, but Hitler ruled about 12 years.

The reign of antichrist is short because it needs to be short. Jesus said of these 3.5 years, which start just as the antichrist declares himself to be god in the temple:

46

*"For then shall be great tribulation, such as was not since the beginning of the world to this time, no, nor ever shall be. **And except those days should be shortened**, there should no flesh be saved: but for the elect's sake those days shall be shortened." – Mat 24:21-22*

(Rev. 17:11)

And the beast that was, and is not, even he is the eighth, and is of the seven, and goeth into perdition.

"And the beast that was, and is not, even he is the eighth, and is of the seven, and goeth into perdition..."

This verse is where we will find confirmation of the view that the beast's coming out of the bottomless pit in verse 8 is a reference to the antichrist's resurrection.

Notice first the similarity to this phrase in verse 11 and the one we looked at earlier in Revelation 17:8:

> *Rev 17:8 The beast that thou sawest was, and is not; and shall ascend out of the bottomless pit, and go into perdition.*
>
> *Rev 17:11 And the beast that was, and is not, even he is the eighth, and is of the seven, and goeth into perdition.*

The difference here is the middle of these two verses (the part about the resurrection). In 17:8, it describes the resurrection as "ascending out of the bottomless pit. "

In verse 11, the part that says "even he is the eighth and is of the seven" is not only being used to convey the same thing (that is the resurrection portion of his chronology), but as we will see, it is also giving us more information about this king.

This phrase **"even he is the eighth, and is of the seven"** is saying that though there are only seven kings, there will be eight reigns. That is, one of

47

these kings will rule twice. The resurrection of antichrist explains how there can be eight reigns and only seven kings. This is almost universally considered to be speaking of a resurrection of one of the dead seven kings to rule twice. In other words, he will be the eighth king while never ceasing to be the one of the seven kings.

So this provides great credibility to the earlier interpretation that this phrase is a technical title of the beast in Revelation 13 and that the "bottomless pit" in verse 8 is a reference to the beast's resurrection. Just as the phrase "**even he is the eighth, and is of the seven**" is a reference to the resurrection, and that all of it is packaged in an **identical word structure**, so we can be confident of our interpretation that this is a title of the antichrist that refers to his most identifiable trait, his apparent resurrection.

As a side note many people might ask, "Does Satan have the power to raise people from the dead?" I do not believe that he does, but I do think the antichrist is really raised from the dead. For more on this, I would suggest an article on this point called:

"Can Satan Raise The Dead? Toward A Biblical View of the Beast's Wound" by Gregory H. Harris.[6] He is a Professor of Bible Exposition and I would recommend this paper if you are interested. I agree with its overall premise but would probably disagree on some of the finer points.

(Rev 17:12)

And the ten horns which thou sawest are ten kings, which have received no kingdom as yet; but receive power as kings one hour with the beast.

In our verse we see that the beast has seven heads, but also ten horns. We are not told exactly how these horns are distributed on the seven heads or if they are even on the seven heads at all. We don't know if six of the heads have one horn and the seventh has four horns or if they have some other arrangement.

I think when we consider the following passages we will find that these ten horns are working with the final head. So if I were to make a guess, these horns are either all on one head – the seventh one, or possibly not on the heads at all, but some other part of the body.

I also say this because the fourth beast of Daniel 7:7-8 also has ten horns, and that beast is widely considered to be associated with the antichrist.

Let's consider this symbolism so we can get our bearings in this difficult passage. The seven heads of the beast are seven kings, and now we are told that the horns of this beast are also kings. So what is this talking about? Let's read ahead so we can get the context and find the relationship of these kings to the antichrist according to the angel. This will help us make an informed decision.

> *"And the ten horns which thou sawest are ten kings, which have received no kingdom as yet; but receive power as kings one hour with the beast. These have one mind, and shall give their power and strength unto the beast. These shall make war with the Lamb, and the Lamb shall overcome them: for he is Lord of lords, and King of kings: and they that are with him are called, and chosen, and faithful. And he saith unto me, 'The waters which thou sawest, where the whore sitteth, are peoples, and multitudes, and nations, and tongues. And the ten horns which thou sawest upon the beast, these shall hate the whore, and shall make her desolate and naked, and shall eat her flesh, and burn her with fire. For God hath put in their hearts to fulfil his will, and to agree, and give their kingdom unto the beast, until the words of God shall be fulfilled.'" – Rev 17:12-17*

So it seems what we have here is one super king – a supreme dictator – who is the final, yet future, head of the antichrist beast, and has ten other kings under his total authority. So part of the point of this symbolism of the horns on the beast is speaking of a consolidation of power of some kind. The purpose for this consolidation is very interesting and we will talk about that when we get to those verses. But the symbolism here of the ten horns on the beast is one main ruler ruling over others, who willingly give their authority to the dictator, who then uses them to do his bidding.

Before we move on, I would like to briefly talk about the book of Daniel. I take a slightly different view on Daniel 2 and Daniel 7. I think that all four of the beasts in Daniel 7 may be contemporary with the antichrist (as opposed to them lining up directly with the kingdoms of Daniel 2). I think that if this is true, there is much more detail that we can know about the end times scenario than has previously been considered. You can see the studies I did on Daniel 2 and 7 at http://bibleprophecytalk.com.

"...which have received no kingdom as yet; but receive power as kings one hour with the beast. "

First, please notice that this is making a distinction between kings and kingdoms quite boldly. It says: **"ten kings, which have received no kingdom as yet**." This is a strong rebuke to those who try to make the references to kings in these chapters mean kingdoms because of their various presuppositions. John demonstrates that if he or the angel who he is recording wants to say kingdoms instead of kings, they are quite willing and capable of doing so.

These kings are directly tied to the beast. It says that they only rule for **"one hour with the beast**." We will talk in more detail about their kingdoms and how they give away their power to the beast as we look at the next verses where we are given more information about this.

We will take the next two verses together:

(Rev 17:13-14)

These have one mind, and shall give their power and strength unto the beast. These shall make war with the Lamb, and the Lamb shall overcome them: for he is Lord of lords, and King of kings: and they that are with him are called, and chosen, and faithful.

These shall make war with the Lamb

Here is one of the reasons these kings are given power: that is to war against the Lamb, who is of course Jesus Christ. This battle is referring to Armageddon. This may help explain the idea of them ruling for only one hour. By the time of the battle of Armageddon things are looking pretty grim for the antichrist. This would be the final attempt at preventing the return of

Christ to take His throne.

"...and shall give their power and strength..."

I'm not entirely sure that these kings ever do get kingdoms, but they do have some kind of assets that are utilized by the beast. It says here that they give their **power and strength** to the beast for this mission of warring against the Lamb.

Revelation 19 is a picture of this battle of Armageddon:

> *"And out of his mouth goeth a sharp sword, that with it he should smite the nations: and he shall rule them with a rod of iron: and he treadeth the winepress of the fierceness and wrath of Almighty God. And he hath on his vesture and on his thigh a name written, KING OF KINGS, AND LORD OF LORDS." – Rev 19:15-16*

So we see here a clear reference to Armageddon again, and as we compare the different Scriptures about these kings and the final battle they are drawn to fight, my hope is that we are getting a better understanding of who these kings are.

(Rev 17:15)

And he saith unto me, 'The waters which thou sawest, where the whore sitteth, are peoples, and multitudes, and nations, and tongues.

"The waters which thou sawest..."

The angel is giving the interpretation of the waters that John saw the whore on.

"... [The waters] are peoples, and multitudes, and nations, and tongues."

This idea of sitting on peoples, multitudes, nations, and tongues is a way to say that the city of Mystery Babylon rules over many and has great power and authority. This is consistent with the later descriptions of her actions in the next chapter and with her relationship to the other kings of the earth and other nations.

The same language is used when Jeremiah talks about the destruction of actual Babylon in Jeremiah 51:13:

> **"O thou that dwellest upon many waters**, *abundant in treasures, thine end is come, and the measure of thy covetousness." – Jer 51:13*

You will see many similar things like this in Jeremiah 51.

In fact I think this is one of the main reasons why Mystery Babylon is called **Mystery** Babylon, because she shares not only the city of Babylon's former power over nations, but also shares her worship of false gods and, ultimately, Babylon's pattern of judgment, detailed in Jeremiah 51.

I have, of course, been detailing in our study the possibility of the last days city of Jerusalem being Mystery Babylon – the city that rules many nations in the time of the antichrist.

This is an extremely important part of this theory and so it is about time I address it.

It should be noted that Jews and Christians both believe that Jerusalem will be the capital city of the world in the messianic age. The book of Zechariah is just one of many places in the Bible where this promise is made:

> *"Then shall the Lord go forth ... and His feet shall stand in that day upon the mount of Olives, which is before Jerusalem on the east ... and it shall come to pass, that every one that is left of all the nations which came against Jerusalem shall go up from year to year to worship the King, the Lord of hosts, and to keep the feast of tabernacles." (Zech. 12:3, 4, 16, 17)*

You will find that glimpses of Jerusalem's future as world capital are sprinkled all though the Psalms and the major and minor prophets. Jewish people have been waiting for thousands of years for someone to make

Jerusalem the world capital, just as their Scriptures promise will come to pass.

Here are some specific examples:

> *And it shall come to pass that everyone who is left of all the nations which came against Jerusalem shall go up from year to year to worship the King, the LORD of hosts, and to keep the Feast of Tabernacles. - Zec 14:16*

> *Then they shall bring all your brethren for an offering to the LORD out of all nations, on horses and in chariots and in litters, on mules and on camels, to My holy mountain Jerusalem," says the LORD, "as the children of Israel bring an offering in a clean vessel into the house of the LORD. - Isa 66:20*

> *And it shall come to pass That from one New Moon to another, And from one Sabbath to another, All flesh shall come to worship before Me," says the LORD. - Isa 66:23*

I think that our verse, Revelation 17:15, and others like it show that the antichrist will succeed in doing this to an extent, as he masquerades as their Messiah. He will try to make Jerusalem the uncontested world capital.

If you understand this point, then the next chapter about the people making pilgrimages and bringing gifts to the city of Mystery Babylon as if it were the city of the Messianic age, and as if the antichrist were the Messiah, will make a lot more sense to you.

People will try to use this verse about her sitting on waters which are nations to say that the seven- headed beast which she sits on represents kingdoms not kings.

Some are opposed to the waters being what the beast, **along with** the woman atop him, are sitting on. They would say, "Well, it says she sits on waters and it says she sits on a beast, so the beast and the waters must be the same." They would say that this verse defines the beast itself, as opposed to the waters that both the woman and the beast sit on. To say it another way, they are saying that the waters here **are** the beast.

I think this is wrong for two reasons. One, it's more logical to assume that she is sitting on a seven- headed beast and **both of them** are sitting on the waters – that is, ruling over the "peoples and nations," etc. In other words, the city of Jerusalem (the woman) and the beast she rides (the antichrist) are both sitting on (ruling) many peoples and nations.

Not only is this consistent with what we just looked at about the ten-horned kings, who give their authority to the beast, but it also connects to Revelation chapter 13 where we see that the seven- headed, ten-horned antichrist beast comes out of the sea, a consistent idiom for peoples and nations. He is not the sea itself in Revelation 13. In fact, that chapter makes it very clear, in my opinion, that he is a human king.

(Rev 17:16)

And the ten horns which thou sawest upon the beast, these shall hate the whore, and shall make her desolate and naked, and shall eat her flesh, and burn her with fire.

This is a very interesting development. The ten kings who we saw earlier are subordinate to the antichrist and are used to go to war against God, and are also used to destroy the city of Mystery Babylon. So the antichrist here turns on the woman. We will see later that although the kings who do this are under the complete control of the antichrist, it is ultimately God who causes this to happen for the purpose of His Judgment.

Interestingly, this verse is the fulfillment of a detailed prophecy about Jerusalem in the Old Testament book of Ezekiel. Let's take a look:

> *"Again the word of the LORD came to me, saying, 'Son of man,* **cause Jerusalem to know her abominations...**" – Eze 16:1-2

You can see from verses 1 and 2 that this prophecy is about Jerusalem. It says:

*"And I will judge you as women who break wedlock or shed blood are judged; I will bring blood upon you in fury and jealousy. **I will also give you into their hand,** and they shall throw down your shrines and break down your high places. They shall also **strip you of your clothes,** take your beautiful jewelry, and leave you **naked and bare. They shall also bring up an assembly against you,** and they shall stone you with stones and thrust you through with their swords. **They shall burn your houses with fire,** and execute judgments on you in the sight of many women; and I will make you cease **playing the harlot,** and you shall no longer hire lovers." - Eze 16:38-41*

This is exactly fulfilled in our verse back in Revelation 17:15.

Here God says He will give Jerusalem into their hand. So even though the agent of destruction has evil intent, God will use them to carry out His righteous judgment on Jerusalem. You can see the same language being used here as in our verse. They strip her naked and burn her with fire, all because of her "playing the harlot" with false gods.

It should be noted that these earthly kings only constitute a small portion of her destructions. She is also judged by earthquakes and fire from heaven *in addition* to whatever these kings do. I would also submit that the ultimate judgment of Mystery Babylon and the Battle of Armageddon take place at the same time, or very close to one another. I also think they will happen at the same place, i.e., Jerusalem.

For more on this possibility, see a paper called: *"A Big Problem: Where is Har Magedon? An Examination of Revelation 16:16.*

But for now, all you need to know is that although the antichrist turns on the city of Mystery Babylon and uses his lackey kings to plunder her, it is by no means the only judgment she receives according to the seventh bowl judgment and parallel passages.

(Rev 17:17)

For God hath put in their hearts to fulfill his will, and to agree, and give their kingdom unto the beast, until the words of God shall be fulfilled.

"...For God hath put in their hearts to fulfill his will..."

This shows the sovereignty of God in all this. That God is the ultimate force behind this judgment, whether these kings know it or not, is made even clearer in the next chapter which says:

> *"Therefore, shall her plagues come in one day, death, and mourning, and famine; and she shall be utterly burned with fire: **for strong is the Lord God who judgeth her**." – Rev 18:8*

"...And to agree, and give their kingdom unto the beast, until the words of God shall be fulfilled..."

Again this hearkens back to the fact that these ten kings give their power and authority to the beast. Here it says that they collectively have a kingdom, not plural kingdoms. This is interesting and may indicate that the ten kings are representatives of one collective kingdom. This may also explain why they didn't have a kingdom "yet" in verse 12 and why they were only said to give power and authority in verse 13.

(Rev 17:18)

And the woman which thou sawest is that great city, which reigneth over the kings of the earth.

This is a very important verse to study in the process of trying to figure out who Mystery Babylon is. We are told point blank by the angel that this woman is a **city**. The views that try to interpret her to mean something else, such as an allegorical source of spiritual and economic evil, are disregarding the sureness of the angel's interpretation of John's vision.

All through Scripture when interpretations of a vision are given, they are pretty straightforward. It is, therefore, unlikely that the angel would tell John that he was going to interpret his vision and then give him an interpretation that he was not supposed to accept. It would also be inconsistent with the angel's other interpretations in this chapter.

The angel gets specific. He says it is **"that great city, which reigneth over the kings of the earth."**

Now we know from verse 15 that Mystery Babylon will sit over many nations and peoples and tongues. But I think the problem that many commentators have here is that they try to look around their current era and consider which city rules over the earth in their day.

This tendency to look to our surroundings as opposed to the future for fulfillment of this passage has caused a lot of poor interpretations in this writer's opinion.

Considering the antichrist is supposed to set up a world government that most of us would agree is in the future, why would we feel the need to have the passages about his world government capital city fulfilled in the past? The temptation has been too great to resist for most commentators in my library.

"…great city…"

I am under the impression that the Bible would not like us to speculate on this point, and one of the many ways it gives us the answer to this question is by the use of this term **"great city."**

The phrase "great city" is used ten times in the book of Revelation, and every time it refers to the city of Jerusalem. Many people would violently disagree with me on that because they don't see Mystery Babylon (which is called the great city) as Jerusalem.

Let's set aside, for the time, the instances of the phrase "great city" used to refer to Mystery Babylon and only talk about references to the great city where it is absolutely undisputed that it is talking about Jerusalem:

> *"And their dead bodies shall lie in the street of **the great city**, which spiritually is called Sodom and Egypt, **where also our Lord was crucified.**" - Rev 11:8*

Obviously, the city where our Lord was crucified is Jerusalem. No one would deny that. Some commentators concede this point begrudgingly, knowing the problem it creates.

I would also call your attention to the definite article "ho" in the Greek here as in **THE** great city. This ensures we know that Jerusalem is considered by John to have a title of "the great city."

The fact that John uses this phrase "great city," which he uses earlier to define Jerusalem during the time of the two witnesses after they were killed by antichrist is very strong evidence in favor of the interpretation that Mystery Babylon is Jerusalem.

But these "great city" references show that Mystery Babylon is Jerusalem in another way as well. Revelation 16:19 distinguishes the "great city" from the cities of the nations.

> *And **the great city** was divided into three parts, **and the cities of the nations fell**: and great Babylon came in remembrance before God, to give unto her the cup of the wine of the fierceness of his wrath. - Rev 16:19*

Revelationcommentary.org states:
> *"[This] is the second proof that 'the great city' refers to Jerusalem. "The cities of the nations" (Gentiles) is in contrast to 'the great city (Jews).'"*

So to clarify this part, the word Gentiles and nations are almost interchangeable. There are two types of cities in the world if you want to look at it from a Jewish perspective: Jerusalem and the Gentile cities. In this verse, Mystery Babylon is contrasted with the cities of the nations, which suggests that it is not a Gentile nation.

Some who recognize the significance of Revelation 16:19 try to make the reference to Babylon here be a third entity in the discussion.

In other words, they say that "the great city," which they would concede is Jerusalem, is split into three parts, and the cities of the nations also fell, **AND** Babylon was mentioned as a third party.

Most would say that only two parties are in view here: the great city divided into three parts, and the cities of the nations. The following mention of "Great Babylon" is in reference to the "Great city" mentioned just before.

Other translations agree, especially the newer ones. They connect the great city in the first part to great Babylon.

> *(NET) "The[60] great city was split into three parts and the cities of the nations[61] collapsed.[62] So[63] Babylon the great was remembered before God, and was given the cup[64] filled with the wine made of God's furious wrath."[65]*

> *Here [63] καί (kai) has been translated as "so" to indicate the implied result of Babylon's misdeeds (see Rev 14:8).*

Another new Bible that is set to be completed later this year says:

> *(ISV-v2.0) "The great city was split into three parts, and the cities of the nations fell.* **God remembered to give Babylon** *the Great the cup of wine filled with the fury of his wrath."*

The NET Bible renders this, "**So Babylon....**" The ISV renders it, "**God remembered to give Babylon....**" That is to say that it did not introduce a new character here but rather it gives more information about the first character mentioned.

The simple version of this is that the last verse of Revelation 17 calls Mystery Babylon the "Great city," a term that is used to very directly identify the Jerusalem of the antichrist by the same author in the same book using a definite article to indicate a title or at least a very definite identification with the phrase.

Lament Over Fallen Babylon

(Rev 18:1)

And after these things I saw another angel come down from heaven, having great power; and the earth was lightened with his glory.

"And after these things…"

"After these things" basically refers to the events of the previous chapter, chapter 17, where we see John's vision and its interpretation by the angel. This phrase, "after these things," signals a new vision unit.

> **Chapter 17** declared the "judgment of the mystery Babylon." The objects of God's judgment, the woman and the beast she rides, were also described.

> **Chapter 18** will have somewhat similar themes, but it will spend a lot of extra time on the wealth of the city at the time of the antichrist's rule.

"…I saw another angel come down from heaven…"

So the angel that will be speaking at this point is not the same one that gave the interpretation of John's vision in the previous chapter. The previous angel was one of the seven that poured out the last seven bowl judgments (17:1).

This angel is different in many ways. One notable way is that, unlike the previous angel, it does not speak to John directly. John basically overhears the declaration that the angel speaks and records it. The angel seems unconcerned or unaware that John is even present. This could either be a type of drama put on for John's benefit, or perhaps John is overseeing actual events that will take place in the spiritual realm at the time of the harlot city's judgment.

"…having great power; and the earth was lightened with his glory."

This angel is described with some provocative language. It says it has great power. We are not told how John knows this. Perhaps it is evident from its appearance or some other quality.

It is tempting to say this is a picture of Christ because of the idea of the angel's glory lighting the earth, but it is not necessary, as the idea of an angel having illuminating glory, or "doxa" is mentioned in Ezek 9:3 and Heb 9:5. In both cases, a cherub is described. Cherubs spend their time in the throne room of God and so one theory could be that they are shining with the glory just like Moses' face shone when he spent time on Mount Sinai in the very near presence of God (Exo 34:29). So this could simply be a particularly high ranking angel or a cherub.

A point that strengthens this view is that in verse 4, we hear a separate voice from heaven saying, "come out of her my people," which seems to be the voice of Christ (see verse 4 notes). This would mean that this angel is probably not Christ, but a high-ranking angel.

(Rev 18:2)

And he cried mightily with a strong voice, saying, Babylon the great is fallen, is fallen, and is become the habitation of devils, and the hold of every foul spirit, and a cage of every unclean and hateful bird.

It is interesting to note that the last verse of the previous chapter (17:18) was where the first angel concluded its interpretation of John's vision by declaring that the woman was an actual city. Now, in Chapter 18, it begins to refer to Mystery Babylon in this sense with a geographical location. Here it talks of it being a habitation of devils. Later it will speak of merchants bringing goods to it.

While it continues to use the symbolic imagery of the harlot woman to describe Mystery Babylon (18:7), it much more frequently talks of Mystery Babylon as if the reader by now understands that it is a physical city on earth, just as the angel said it was.

"…And he cried mightily with a strong voice…"

The second angel is said to have a strong voice or "megas phone" in the Greek. Earlier in Revelation chapter 5, John described another angel with the phrase "megas phone" when he is having a vision of the throne room of God:

> *"And I saw in the right hand of him that sat on the throne a book written within and on the backside, sealed with seven seals. And I saw a strong angel proclaiming with a **loud voice**, 'Who is worthy to open the book, and to loose the seals thereof?'" – Rev 5:1-2*

Because this angel is apparently in such close proximity to the throne, and it is described with the same strong voice, it lends a measure of credibility to the earlier interpretation that the angel of Revelation 18 is a cherub, or at least of the same quality and rank as the angel in our current verse.

"…saying, Babylon the great is fallen, is fallen…"

The angel seems to be hearkening back to the familiar phrase used in the various prophecies of the old city of Babylon's destruction:

> *"And, behold, here cometh a chariot of men, with a couple of horsemen. And he answered and said, **Babylon is fallen, is fallen**; and all the graven images of her gods he hath broken unto the ground." – Isa 21:9*

John F. Walvoord, a well-known theologian and author notes:

> *"The repetition of the verb 'is fallen,' found in the aorist tense, indicates a sudden event viewed as completed, though the context would indicate a future event."[7]*

It seems that what's happening with this phrase is that the destruction of Mystery Babylon is indicated here as being imminent – that is, it hasn't happened at this point, but it is now on its way or imminent. The context of the rest of this chapter supports this conclusion, as Walvoord also noted.

"...and is become the habitation of devils, and the hold of every foul spirit, and a cage of every unclean and hateful bird..."

Here John makes it clear by the use of the terms "devils" and "foul spirits" that this city is home to multiple demonic entities. The idea of a "hateful bird" is also an indication of demonic beings. Actual birds are not "hateful" even if they are birds of prey or scavengers. In addition, birds are used in other places to refer to demonic beings, or at least the work of Satan (Mark 4:3-4, 13-15).

There is a very interesting parallel to the devils and birds lodging in a city which can be seen in the passages referring to Babylon's destruction in the Old Testament:

> *"And thorns shall come up in her palaces, nettles and brambles in the fortresses thereof: and it shall be **an habitation of dragons**, and a **court for owls**." – Isa 34:13*

When we read on we find more interesting points:

> *"The wild beasts of the desert shall also meet with the wild beasts of the island, and the satyr shall cry to his fellow; the screech owl also shall rest there, and find for herself a place of rest. There shall the great owl make her nest, and lay, and hatch, and gather under her shadow: there shall the vultures also be gathered, every one with her mate." – Isa 34:14-15*

I think that there are two possibilities here. This could be referring to the utter desolation that the city will be reduced to after its destruction. That is, it will only be inhabitable by beasts and birds. However, I think, because of the explicit language John uses here about demonic beings, that this may refer to the gathering of demons that would take place if Satan, through the antichrist, makes a particular city his capital city at the end times. It would be a kind of gathering place or abode of these beings.

Revelationcommentary.org says of this idea:

"The Harlot City is the home or lair of the demons…. These are issues, which contribute to the wickedness of this harlot/city. Everything that the city stood for has been perverted. Evil in its worst form makes its home in God's holy city. She is a harlot destined to destruction."

(Rev 18:3)

For all nations have drunk of the wine of the wrath of her fornication, and the kings of the earth have committed fornication with her, and the merchants of the earth are waxed rich through the abundance of her delicacies.

"For all nations…"

This is referring to the fact that the whole world is enticed into worshiping the antichrist. We see references to the **"all nations"** phrase in relation to the antichrist in several places:

> *"And I saw one of his heads as it were wounded to death; and his deadly wound was healed: and **all the world** wondered after the beast." – Rev 13:3*

> *"And **all that dwell upon the earth** shall worship him, whose names are not written in the book of life of the Lamb slain from the foundation of the world." – Rev 13:8*

> *"And he **causeth all, both small and great, rich and poor, free and bond**, to receive a mark in their right hand, or in their foreheads…" – Rev 13:16*

"…have drunk of the wine of the wrath of her fornication…"

Other translations perhaps render the sense of it better; for instance the ESV says:

> *"For all nations have drunk the wine of **the passion** of her*

65

[fornication]...”

The idea is that she herself is so deceived by the antichrist that she passionately promotes him and worships him as her messiah, her long awaited king and husband. So intense is her fornication that the entire world is somehow drawn in to be deceived by his seductive power as well.

The phrase "**kings of the earth**." Here it seems to almost be saying the same thing as the first part of this verse – that is, that all the nations drink of her fornication. It seems to be restating this, as Scripture will do from time to time, when it says the kings of the earth commit fornication. In other words, not just the people of the earth, but the rulers of those people will also be engaged in this fornication.

Some other passages in Scripture seem to suggest that these kings have more of a financial interest in the fornication than a religious interest. The kings seem to have similar motives as the merchants in relation to the Mystery Babylon city. For instance, later on it says of these kings:

> *"And the kings of the earth, who have committed fornication **and lived deliciously with her**, shall bewail her, and lament for her, when they shall see the smoke of her burning." – Rev 18:9*

The phrase "**lived deliciously with her**" seems to suggest that the kings have similar motives as the merchants who are mentioned next. There is a financial interest for them, as there will apparently be a lot of revenue to be made out of all the people of the world being forced to pay tribute to the antichrist.

I think it would be wrong to conclude that the **kings of the earth** mentioned here are exact matches to the ten kings that are used to destroy the city and to war against the descent of Christ at Armageddon. Although there may be some of the same kings involved, I think the intention here in verse 3 is more broad, and suggestive of the rulers of the entire world, not just ten specific ones used for a specific purpose, as is the case with the ten kings mentioned in chapter 17.

"...and the merchants of the earth are waxed rich through the abundance of her delicacies."

These merchants are going to be discussed at great length at the end of this chapter, and I am going to spend quite a lot of time discussing them. So I will not spend all that much time here except to simply say that the merchants of the earth will prosper during the time of celebration over the antichrist as if he is the Messiah.

Come out of her my people

(Rev 18:4)

And I heard another voice from heaven, saying, 'Come out of her, my people, that ye be not partakers of her sins, and that ye receive not of her plagues.

"...another voice from heaven..."

This is probably the voice of Jesus Christ, because this voice has people that belong to it. All believers have been given to Christ by God as His inheritance (John 6:37, 39-40, 10:27-28; Heb 2:13.)

In addition, in the next verse this voice from heaven refers to "God" when it says, "God hath remembered her iniquities." This gives me confidence that the voice must be that of Jesus Christ. Another clue is that this is "**another voice**," i.e., not the powerful angel who shines, which we saw earlier. We can therefore also be confident of the interpretation that that previous angel, (the one that shines with a loud voice), is not Jesus Christ either, but rather some high-ranking angel.

"...saying, Come out of her, my people, that ye be not partakers of her sins, and that ye receive not of her plagues..."

The **plagues** that Mystery Babylon is about to be given refers to its destruction, a destruction that this chapter says will happen very quickly (18:10, 17, 19.)

I believe that the idea that His people need to come out of the city in order not to receive its judgments is a direct reference to the Mount of Olives being split just before the judgment of Jerusalem which allows the faithful to flee the city before the final bowl of wrath is poured out (which destroys the city of Mystery Babylon).

We see a picture of this "coming out of her" in Zechariah 14:

> *"And his feet shall stand in that day upon the mount of Olives, which is before Jerusalem on the east, and the mount of Olives shall cleave in the midst thereof toward the east and toward the west, and there shall be a very great valley; and half of the mountain shall remove toward the north, and half of it toward the south. **And ye shall flee to the valley of the mountains**; for the valley of the mountains shall reach **unto Azal: yea, ye shall flee, like as ye fled from before the earthquake in the days of Uzziah king of Judah**: and the LORD my God shall come, and all the saints with thee." – Zec 14:4 -5*

We can compare this verse with its fulfillment in Revelation 16:

> *"And the seventh angel poured out his vial into the air; and there came a great voice out of the temple of heaven, from the throne, saying, 'It is done.' And there were voices, and thunders, and lightnings; and there was **a great earthquake**, such as was not since men were upon the earth, so mighty an earthquake, and so great. And **the great city was divided into three parts**, and the cities of the nations fell: and **great Babylon came in remembrance before God, to give unto her the cup of the wine of the fierceness of his wrath**. And every island fled away, and the mountains were not found. And there fell upon men a great hail out of heaven, every stone about the weight of a talent: and men blasphemed God because of the plague of the hail; for the **plague** thereof was exceeding great." – Rev 16:17-21*

So the people that He is calling out here probably were never participating in the sin of Mystery Babylon, as is sometimes implied when people use this phrase, "come out of her my people." His people are simply being called to get out of the city because it is about to be judged for its sins – sins they probably had no part in.

(Rev 18:5)

For her sins have reached unto heaven, and God hath remembered her iniquities

I have a somewhat interesting view of this idea of the fullness of sins, or the idea that sins reach to heaven. I think that a very biblical idea is that some nations have a kind of allotment or threshold of evil, particularly that of spilled innocent blood, before God judges them.

For instance, in Genesis God tells Abraham that He won't give him his inheritance of the land of Israel yet because the current inhabitants' (the Amorites) sin was not yet full:

> *"But in the fourth generation they shall come hither again: for the iniquity of the Amorites is **not yet full.**" – Gen 15:16*

We see a similar idea in Daniel when it says that the real reason that the four kingdoms which developed after Greece died out, is because they had reached their sin allotments:

> *"And in the latter time of their kingdom, **when the transgressors are come to the full**, a king of fierce countenance, and understanding dark sentences, shall stand up." – Dan 8:23*

Scholars almost universally agree that this allotment or fullness of sins for nations is what Jesus was talking about when He said the following to the men of Jerusalem:

> *"Wherefore ye be witnesses unto yourselves, that ye are the children of them which killed the prophets. **Fill ye up then the measure of your fathers.** Ye serpents, ye generation of vipers, how can ye escape the damnation of hell? Wherefore, behold, I send unto you prophets, and wise men, and scribes: and some of them ye shall kill and crucify; and some of them shall ye scourge in your synagogues, and persecute them from city to city: That upon you may come all the righteous blood shed upon the earth, from the blood of righteous Abel unto the blood of Zacharias son of Barachias, whom ye slew*

between the temple and the altar." – Mat 23:31-35

It should also be remembered that the persecution the antichrist ordered at the midpoint of the seven- year period will be the worst persecution of all time (Mat 24:15-22). But in addition to this, we see that the actual killing of Old Testament prophets for Jerusalem is not over yet either. We see at least one more future instance of this occurring with the two witnesses.

> *"And their dead bodies shall lie in the street of the great city, which spiritually is called Sodom and Egypt, where also our Lord was crucified." – Rev 11:8*

It's quite possible that this event brings Jerusalem very near to its fullness of sins allotted by God, as it occurs on the very last day of the seventieth week of Daniel, just thirty days before the destruction of Jerusalem.

"...God hath remembered her iniquities..."

This should also be seen as God's longsuffering with people and nations. He does not desire for any to perish, but that all should come to repentance (2 Peter 3:9). We see that even with Nineveh God accepted its repentance, even though He said the same thing of it: *"their wickedness is come up before me."* But just like Jerusalem, God sent prophets to warn them. He gave them chance after chance and was longsuffering. God is blameless when judgment must come to people or nations.

(Rev 18:6)

Reward her even as she rewarded you, and double unto her double according to her works: in the cup which she hath filled fill to her double.

"Reward her even as she rewarded you..."

Jesus, the voice from heaven, is talking to His people here, saying that Mystery Babylon will be judged according to what it has done to His people.

"...and double unto her double according to her works: in the cup which she hath filled fill to her double."

The idea of a double portion of judgment is very consistent in the Old Testament (Isa 40:2, 61:7; Jer 16:18, 17:18; Zec 9:12,) often in reference to Jerusalem.

Jeremiah 16:18 is of note because, in context, this is speaking of a future double judgment, one that happens after they will be gathered back into the land after the diaspora:

> *"And first I will recompense their iniquity and their sin **double**; because they have defiled my land, they have filled mine inheritance with the carcases of their detestable and abominable things." – Jer 16:18*

(Rev 18:7)

How much she hath glorified herself, and lived deliciously, so much torment and sorrow give her: for she saith in her heart, I sit a queen, and am no widow, and shall see no sorrow.

"How much she hath glorified herself and lived deliciously..."

She is exalting herself here. Revelationcommentary.org points out that Luke 14:11a says, "For whosoever exalteth himself shall be abased...."

The Greek word rendered here **"deliciously"** is only used twice in the NT – here and a few verses later to describe the lifestyle of the kings of the earth as a result of their fornication with the beast and his capital city.

At this time Jerusalem will be exalted as the city above all others. It will be the epicenter of the worship of the antichrist and all that is associated with it. There will be nothing to compare this time with in history. However, this will no doubt pale in comparison to the real thing – that is, Christ's actual rule from the temple in Zion, which the antichrist is obviously trying to imitate here.

"…for she saith in her heart, I sit a queen…"

This verse has come up many times in our study, because it's a great picture of the fact that Mystery Babylon herself is just as deceived by the antichrist as those she entices to worship him. She says her place on top of the beast is **as a queen** – that is, she believes she has found her king – her long awaited Messiah. In fact, in Jewish eschatology, the title of the man they await is "the anointed king."

"…and am no widow, and shall see no sorrow."

These two ideas – that she is no widow and shall see no sorrow – are possibly references to her confidence in the beast and his ability to defend her.

It should be noted that after the antichrist rises from the dead, people say of him:

> *"…and they worshiped the beast, saying, 'Who is like unto the beast? Who is able to make war with him?'" – Rev 13:4b*

The attitude that Jerusalem takes during this time is exactly the same as Babylon before its destruction, as we see in:

> *"Therefore hear now this, thou that art given to pleasures, that dwellest carelessly, that sayest in thine heart, I am, and none else beside me;* ***I shall not sit as a widow, neither shall I know the loss of children…"*** *– Isa 47:8*

(Rev 18:8)

Therefore shall her plagues come in one day, death, and mourning, and famine; and she shall be utterly burned with fire: for strong is the Lord God who judgeth her.

"Therefore shall her plagues come in one day…"

This **"therefore"** is here to connect this verse to the previous verse, which showed the woman saying "and [I] shall see no sorrow."

So it is contrasting her belief that she will not see any sorrow, or her perceived security with her husband the beast, with the actual fact that she will be judged in just one day. This is also why it is said later: **"for strong *is* the Lord God who judgeth her."** It is saying that even though she thinks no harm can come to her or the beast, God will do it very easily.

"...one day..."

The idea that her destruction comes suddenly is a consistent one. We see this explicitly mentioned in various ways. Phrases like "one day" or "one hour" are used to describe the suddenness of her judgment.

We know from the last bowl judgment that an earthquake will be involved in splitting the city into three parts, so this would seem to support the idea of a very quick judgment.

"...death, and mourning, and famine; and she shall be utterly burned with fire..."

These things will all play some role in her destruction as well. I think that the destruction has at least two phases. The first includes whatever the "ten kings" do. It says in Rev 17:16 that they will **"eat her flesh and burn her with fire**." The second phase is whatever is done to her via the last bowl judgment with the earthquake and great hail.

Words like "fire" and "burning" as well as ideas like people seeing the smoke of her burning are mentioned several times in relation to Mystery Babylon's destruction. Because of this, I feel that fire is the primary agent of destruction, or at least it is the result of the judgment.

(Rev 18:9-10)

And the kings of the earth, who have committed fornication and lived deliciously with her, shall bewail her, and lament for her, when they

shall see the smoke of her burning. Standing afar off for the fear of her torment, saying, Alas, alas that great city Babylon, that mighty city! for in one hour is thy judgment come.

"And the kings of the earth, who have committed fornication and lived deliciously with her, shall bewail her, and lament for her…"

I have already mentioned how this shows that although the **kings of the earth** commit the same religious **fornication** with her, it is the "**AND** lived deliciously" part that is the reason for their mourning here. Later we will see the same lamentation coming from the merchants who also are said to have lived "deliciously" with her.

"…when they shall see the smoke of her burning…"

This phrase is more evidence that the ten kings or 10 horns, which the antichrist uses to burn Mystery Babylon, are not necessarily the "kings of the earth" mentioned. If they were the ones who burned her down, they probably would not be lamenting when they saw her burning.

"Standing afar off for the fear of her torment…"

This suggests that the city's destruction is not something people want to get too close to for some reason. It could be as simple as the fact that it is on fire, but it could be something more significant. We just are not told.

"…saying, 'Alas, alas, that great city Babylon, that mighty city! For in one hour is thy judgment come.'"

The kings note again the quickness of her destruction, and it happens in "one hour" they say. Again, this contrasts their previous view of its perceived might and sustainability with its lightning fast destruction. What they thought was strong was, in actuality, quite weak. They differ here from the previous similar statement made by the voice from heaven in that they do not add: "God is strong." They only are astonished that this event has happened to Mystery Babylon.

The Merchants and Their Goods

(Rev 18:11)

And the merchants of the earth shall weep and mourn over her; for no man buyeth their merchandise any more.

So here we see the merchants are also upset about this. We are told why they are upset as well, and that is because **"no man buyeth their merchandise any more."**

Now in the next two verses we are going to spend a lot of time on the specific items that these merchants used to sell to the capital city of the antichrist.

You should take note that these are not just any merchants.

Revelation 18:15 tells us that the merchants are the merchants of **"THESE things."** Those are the particular items that we are about to study in depth. They are not **all** the merchants of the world, or symbolically representative of the world economy. I believe the primary reason we are told of the specific items sold to Mystery Babylon is so we can be absolutely sure of who she is and what she is doing during the time of her unfaithfulness.

(Rev 18:12)

The merchandise of gold, and silver, and precious stones, and of pearls, and fine linen, and purple, and silk, and scarlet, and all thyine wood, and all manner vessels of ivory, and all manner vessels of most precious wood, and of brass, and iron, and marble

This is the first of two verses that contain items sold to Mystery Babylon.

Let me first give you the overall picture of what I think we are going to see in these verses.

These are mostly items specific to the reinstitution of the sacrificial system and the rebuilding of the temple. They also include various items that are required for the maintenance of the temple system. There are other fascinating items, too. For instance, take a look at this first phrase:

"...gold, and silver, and precious stones..."

Now we will see there are many uses for these items in the temple, and we could make all kinds of connections if we wanted to, but I think we should be careful to make sure we are looking for exact matches, not just general ones. I also think this phrase does have a very interesting exact match.

These words only appear in the same verse three other times in the Bible.

The first instance is in a kind of master list of the things needed to build the temple given to us by David. This is an important verse, and we will see a lot of interesting things in it later on. For now, notice the items are not in the order we have in our verse, that is, "**gold, and silver, and precious stones.**" They are simply included in the items.

> *"Now I have prepared with all my might for the house of my God the **gold** for things to be made of gold, and the silver for things of **silver**, and the brass for things of brass, the iron for things of iron, and wood for things of wood; onyx stones, and stones to be set, glistering stones, and of divers colours, and all manner of **precious stones**, and marble stones in abundance." – 1Ch 29:2*

That's pretty significant, but let's look at the other two instances of these items in the Bible to see if there is a more significant connection.

The next instance is talking about the great wealth of Israel's King Hezekiah. Here it mentions that he made treasuries of silver, gold, and precious stones.

> *"And Hezekiah had exceeding much riches and honour: and he made himself* **treasuries for silver, and for gold, and for precious stones***, and for spices, and for shields, and for all manner of pleasant jewels..." – 2Ch 32:27*

The phrase is pretty close, like in the other one, but it reverses silver and gold and it's also talking about treasuries. It could be a match, but I don't really think so. Let's check the third and last instance of these words.

> *"Neither shall he regard the God of his fathers, nor the desire of women, nor regard any god: for he shall magnify himself above all. But in his estate shall he honour the God of forces: and a god whom his fathers knew not shall he honour with* **gold, and silver, and with precious stones***, and pleasant things." – Dan 11:37-38*

Here we have an exact match with our phrase. In my opinion, it is not a coincidence that it is found not only in a verse that is all about the antichrist, but also in a verse which is also about the items that will be used in the antichrist's fake religious service. I say fake because in verse 37, it says he will not regard any god, but then it says, "BUT in his estate shall he honour... a god... with **gold, and silver, and with precious stones**." So it seems to me that he says one thing and does another.

The main point is that the first phrase listed for items that will be sold to the city of the antichrist, just happens to be the exact same phrase as the items that the antichrist's estate will offer to a god of forces during his reign. This is the only two times in the Bible this exact phrase is used.

"...pearls, and fine linen, and purple, and silk, and scarlet..."

These items also seem to be a part of a set. If you remember when we looked at Rev 17:4, we looked in depth at the "fine linen, purple and scarlet" as one of the most used phrases in the book of Exodus. There it is told how to make the curtains and dividers of the tabernacle, as well as the veil, the priests' clothing, and almost anything else made of cloth that was in service of the tabernacle. They always used this phrase: **"fine linen, purple and scarlet."** We also mentioned the notable lack of the word "blue" in this phrase in Revelation, which the Bible makes clear is a symbol of their right relationship with Him (Num 15:38-41.)

We have talked in this study about how in the Old Testament God speaks of Jerusalem as having dressed herself with precious materials in her youth, but then it describes how she goes astray after other gods and defiles the way God originally dressed her. I mention this because I think the word "**silk**" in our verse is an interesting clue.

Silk is not mentioned in any of the earlier passages about the types of clothing Mystery Babylon wears. In fact, this is the only time the word silk appears in the entire New Testament. It's also rare in the Old Testament, appearing only 3 times. Each mention is important, and I think if we look at them it will confirm that we are on the right track with our interpretation.

The first one is from Proverbs 31. This is the famous proverb about a virtuous woman. It's the great model for women of all ages, and it says here that she wears silk.

The last two times silk is mentioned in the Bible are both in the same chapter, chapter 16 of Ezekiel. This is a chapter we have looked at many times in the course of our study. It is the picture of the city of Jerusalem from God's eyes, where He talks about how in her youth He clothed her as a virtuous woman with silk. In this way, it is a picture of the woman of Proverbs 31.

> "I clothed thee also with broidered work, and shod thee with badgers' skin, and I girded thee about with fine linen, and I covered thee with **silk**." – Eze 16:10

> "Thus wast thou decked with gold and silver; and thy raiment was of fine linen, and **silk**, and broidered work; thou didst eat fine flour, and honey, and oil: and thou wast exceeding beautiful, and thou didst prosper into a kingdom." – Eze 16:13

Now a few verses later we see that she commits adultery; but notice that she retains her original clothing and simply uses it to help her attract men who symbolically represent false gods, as we are told later.

> "'And thy renown went forth among the heathen for thy beauty: **for it was perfect through my comeliness, which I had put upon thee,**' saith the Lord GOD. 'But thou didst trust in thine own beauty, and

playedst the harlot because of thy renown, and pouredst out thy fornications on every one that passed by; his it was.'" – *Eze 16:14-15*

Later we see her using these garments, given to her by God, to further her worship of false gods on high places.

I believe the mention of silk here completes the garments of Mystery Babylon, which are symbolic and also show that she is the one who was decked by God Himself in her youth. In other words, she is Jerusalem. Also, the same language is used to point back to twenty-three mentions of these specific items in the book of Exodus – all items that have to do with service of the temple.

As a side note, I noticed while doing a word search that the only times these phrases like "**fine linen, purple and scarlet**" appear in the same verse is these twenty-three times in Exodus referring to the items in the temple and the priests' clothing. The other two times are interestingly in the book of Revelation talking about Mystery Babylon. I don't think that is a coincidence.

"...thyine wood..."

This one is extremely interesting. This word, **thyine** is not found anywhere else in the Bible. The wood itself is known to be a very expensive and rare wood used in the ancient world for building things such as ornate furniture, doors of temples, musical instruments, and idols.

As I said, this exact word only appears here in the Bible, but some like The Encyclopedia of Biblical literature, Volume 1, connect this wood to algum wood, or sometimes called almug wood, which is found in the Old Testament a few times, although still very rarely.[8]

All five instances of this word algum or almug trees in the Old Testament are referring to the exact same instance. That instance is when Solomon was building the first temple in Jerusalem, and how he had the merchants bring all kinds of materials and wealth to Jerusalem. We will look in depth at this time toward the end of our study, but for now let's notice the use of this particular wood.

> *"And the servants also of Huram, and the servants of Solomon,*
> *which brought gold from Ophir, brought **algum** trees and precious*
> *stones. And the king made of the **algum trees** terraces to the house of*
> *the LORD, and to the king's palace, and harps and psalteries for*
> *singers: and **there were none such seen before in the land of***
> ***Judah.***" – 2Ch 9:10-11

In 1 Kings, we see basically the same thing, but there it calls this wood
"almug," although it is clear it's talking about the same thing as Kings and
Chronicles often do.

So we are told that this wood is used for terraces of the temple and for
musical instruments. Then we are told that it was so rare and precious that it
was not seen in Israel before this time. So we know that it was imported.

If you only noticed one thing about this, I would hope that it would be that
the only time we see this wood used in the Bible is in the context of it being
imported to Jerusalem by merchants for use in the building of the temple.
Though the king used the remainder for himself, it is clear that the temple
was its primary use.

"...vessels of ivory..."

Ivory is also a rare term in the Old Testament, but just like thyine wood, it
shows up at this time of great wealth and building during Solomon's reign.

> *"Moreover the king made a **great throne of ivory**, and overlaid it*
> *with the best gold.... For the king had at sea a navy of Tharshish*
> *with the navy of Hiram: once in three years came the navy of*
> *Tharshish, bringing gold, and silver, **ivory**, and apes, and peacocks.*
> *So king Solomon exceeded all the kings of the earth for riches and*
> *for wisdom.*" – 1Ki 10:18-23

So again we see one of the few references to ivory in the Old Testament is
talking about it being imported to Jerusalem by merchants. Here it is the
merchants of Tharshish to service the king in his overabundant wealth, and it
talks about a great throne being constructed out of ivory.

There is another reference to King Ahab of Israel building an entire palace of ivory during his reign. This is probably where we get the idea of kings living in "ivory towers." I think the connection to the merchants, ivory, the buildup of Jerusalem, and the throne of ivory are all important clues. Again, we will look a little closer at this time of Solomon's kingdom later on.

"...all manner vessels of most precious wood, and of brass, and iron, and marble..."

I am going to take this phrase as a unit. The only other time in Scripture that these words appear in the same verse is 1Ch 29:2. This is where King David lists the items he has acquired for Solomon to build the temple. Though God prevented David from building a temple, he was allowed to gather the materials for Solomon. As you read it, notice that it is almost an exact match of the entire verse of Revelation 18:12, but we are reading it here to show that **precious wood, brass, iron, and marble** are all specifically mentioned.

> *"Now I have prepared with all my might for the house of my God the gold for [things to be made] of gold, and the silver for [things] of silver, and the **brass** for [things] of **brass**, the **iron** for [things] of **iron**, and **wood** for [things] of **wood**; onyx stones, and [stones] to be set, glistering stones, and of divers colours, and all manner of precious stones, and **marble stones** in abundance." – 1Ch 29:2*

It should again be noted that this is an extremely rare collection of words. It is significant when we find the only other verse in Scripture that contains all of these words is all about the temple service. It wouldn't be as meaningful if it only happened once or twice, but as we will see, it continually occurs.

(Rev 18:13)

And cinnamon, and odours, and ointments, and frankincense, and wine, and oil, and fine flour, and wheat, and beasts, and sheep, and horses, and chariots, and slaves, and souls of men.

Here is the next list of items that the merchants sell to Mystery Babylon, the capital city of the antichrist in the end times.

"And cinnamon, and odours, and ointments, and frankincense..."

These first four items should be taken as a set. I believe each word was carefully chosen to make sure we were pointed back to the same chapter in the Old Testament, Exodus chapter 30.

Exodus chapter 30 is where we find instructions regarding temple service, and this is also where we find two specific recipes: one for the incense to be offered on the altar of incense and another for holy anointing oil which was to consecrate priests and kings.

One interesting thing is that after each of these recipes is given, we have a warning about making anything like it.

> *Anointing oil* – *whoever compounds any like it or whoever puts any of it on an outsider shall be cut off from his people – Exo 30:33*

> *Incense/perfume* – *whoever makes any like it to use as perfume shall be cut off from his people – Exo 30:38*

This should show us that these items are exclusively to be used in the service of the temple and its various duties.

Let's look a little closer at the words in our passage and then at the recipes in Exodus 30.

"And cinnamon..."

Cinnamon is another rare word. In fact, this is the only time it is used in the New Testament, and it is used only three times in the Old Testament.

It is used once in Exodus 30 as part of the recipe for the sacred anointing oil. There is also a mention of cinnamon in Proverbs 7 as the adulterous woman who spices her bed while trying to seduce a man. The third is in Song of Solomon when Solomon compares a woman to expensive spices including cinnamon.

If this was the only connection that this list in Revelation 18 had to Exodus 30 (that is that cinnamon is a key ingredient in the holy anointing oil), I might

84

consider this to be a coincidence, but as I mentioned, I think it becomes more and more clear that the words in Revelation 18 were carefully chosen so that we would make this connection to Exodus 30.

"...and odours..."

This word "odors" appears six times in the New Testament, and four of those times are in the book of Revelation. Each time it is referring specifically to incense on the altar of incense – the specific incense used in worshiping God in the temple.

In Exodus 30, the chapter I believe we are being pointed to, this word appears more times than any other chapter. It appears there **seven times**.

"...ointments..."

This word is used in the New Testament in a more general way to refer to the compounds of great value used as perfumes and for anointing. Sometimes they could be as costly as a year's wages or more. This comes up in the New Testament several times.

However, in the Old Testament this takes on a much more specific usage. In fact, according to the Septuagint the corresponding Hebrew word is used just three times in the Old Testament. If you guessed that Exodus 30 was one of those times, you would be right.

In the following passage, it is translated as the word compound.

> *"And thou shalt make it an oil of holy ointment, an ointment* **compound** *after the art of the apothecary: it shall be an holy anointing oil. And thou shalt anoint the tabernacle of the congregation therewith, and the ark of the testimony, And the table and all his vessels, and the candlestick and his vessels, and the altar of incense, And the altar of burnt offering with all his vessels, and the laver and his foot. And thou shalt sanctify them, that they may be most holy: whatsoever toucheth them shall be holy. And thou shalt anoint Aaron and his sons, and consecrate them, that they may minister unto me in the priest's office." – Exo 30:25-30*

Remember this was a compound that was specifically forbidden to be used in any other way than the service of the temple.

"...frankincense..."

The next word, frankincense, is only used twice in the NT – in this verse, and in Matthew when it is referring to the gifts brought to Jesus by the Magi.

In the Old Testament, the first time this word appears is...you guessed it Exodus 30, as a part of the recipe for the holy incense for temple service.

It is also used as a part of the sacrificial offerings, and I believe it serves as a kind of bridge to the next set of items.

"...wine, and oil, and fine flour, and wheat, and beasts, and sheep..."

I am sure these items are meant to go together as a set since they are the exact things needed for the daily offerings at the temple.

Everything we need to know here is found not in Exodus 30, but in the chapter before it, Exodus 29. I would say that this is probably even part of the Exodus 30 passages considering that the chapter breaks are a recent addition.

In Exodus 29, we find instructions for the daily offering below. Compare Revelation 18:13 to this verse:

> *"And with the one **lamb** a tenth deal of **flour** mingled with the fourth part of an hin of beaten **oil**; and the fourth part of an hin of **wine** for a drink offering." – Exo 29:40*

So we see that **lambs, flour, oil**, and **wine** are all mentioned here! Again we have the same pattern. The only times that these words appear in the same verses in Scripture are in Revelation 18:13 and Exodus 29:40.

This is, quite simply, a list of the components of the daily offerings.

It should not be missed that this daily offering is an exceedingly important aspect of the end time scenario, as it is when the daily offering ceases (by the antichrist's sitting in the temple and declaring himself to be God) that the 3.5-year countdown begins. Daniel says this about it:

> *"And from the time that the **daily sacrifice** shall be taken away, and the abomination that maketh desolate set up, there shall be a thousand two hundred and ninety days." – Dan 12:11*

So we know that the daily sacrifice will be instituted again in the time of the antichrist but there is something missing.

"Wheat" and **"beasts"** are mentioned as well in this verse. In Revelation 18:13, it contrasts wheat with flour so there is probably an intended distinction between them, and it contrasts sheep with the general term for beasts as well.

Back in Exodus 29 we find why this distinction is used.

> *"And this is the thing that thou shalt do unto them to hallow them, to minister unto me in the priest's office: Take one young bullock, and two rams without blemish, And unleavened bread, and cakes unleavened tempered with oil, and wafers unleavened anointed with oil: of wheaten flour shalt thou make them." – Exo 29:1-2*

The first verses of this chapter, which is about the daily offerings, start with the necessary preparations in order to make these daily offerings. They had to first consecrate the priests and the altar. One bullock and two rams or **beasts** were needed as well as **wheat** flour. This is the only time wheat is mentioned in conjunction with sacrifice in this chapter.

So **wheat** and **beasts** are added to the list in Revelation 18:13 as an indispensable part of the preparation for daily offerings. So this set of items **(wine, and oil, and fine flour, and wheat, and beasts, and sheep)** represents a shopping list for everything you will need if you plan on making daily offerings in the temple.

"...horses, and chariots, and slaves, and souls of men."

I think this last phrase begins a new class of items sold to Mystery Babylon by the merchants.

"...horses..."

This is an interesting one, too. I think before we can fully understand its significance, we need to take a little detour and look at the life of King Solomon during the time of his building the temple.

In 1 Kings 10, it tells of Solomon's rule, widely considered to be the most prosperous time in Israel's history. You will hear that silver was considered nothing in those days, because there was so much gold, but there is an interesting parallel between everything we have seen so far and this time in Solomon's life.

We will see that it is a time where the entire world is in service to Solomon, but it doesn't seem to end well for him personally. In fact, the next chapter after this says the following of him:

> *"For it was so, when Solomon was old, that his wives turned his heart after other gods; and his heart was not loyal to the LORD his God, as was the heart of his father David. For Solomon went after Ashtoreth the goddess of the Sidonians, and after Milcom the abomination of the Ammonites." – 1 Ki 11:4-5*

It then talks about how he starts to build houses for these gods and is utterly devoted to them. We are not told whether Solomon repented of this or not. I think he probably did, but I have no biblical support for that.

The interesting section that I want to show you is just before these verses about him following other gods. We will start with a verse that I think represents a marker to show when things started to go wrong for Solomon. It says:

> *"The weight of gold that came to Solomon yearly was **six hundred and sixty-six** talents of gold..." – 1 Ki 10:14*

Now, 666 is a pretty interesting number. This is the only other time in the Bible it occurs besides the passage in the book of Revelation. I'm not claiming that this has any real significance as to the mark of the beast, or even that it is a clue of some sort. I only think it's interesting that if you read between this verse and the verses about him going after other gods, you have a section of Scripture that I think is one of the most overlooked types (or prophetic foreshadows) of the antichrist and the time when he will reign in Jerusalem and when these merchants will grow rich of the opulence of the capital city of the antichrist.

> *"The weight of gold that came to Solomon yearly was six hundred and sixty-six talents of gold, besides that from the traveling merchants, from the income of traders, from all the kings of Arabia, and from the governors of the country. And King Solomon made two hundred large shields of hammered gold; six hundred shekels of gold went into each shield. He also made three hundred shields of hammered gold; three minas of gold went into each shield. The king put them in the House of the Forest of Lebanon. Moreover the king made a great throne of ivory, and overlaid it with pure gold. ... nothing like this had been made for any other kingdom. All King Solomon's drinking vessels were gold, and all the vessels of the House of the Forest of Lebanon were pure gold. Not one was silver, for this was accounted as nothing in the days of Solomon. For the king had merchant ships at sea with the fleet of Hiram. Once every three years the merchant ships came bringing gold, silver, ivory, apes, and monkeys. So King Solomon surpassed all the kings of the earth in riches and wisdom. Now all the earth sought the presence of Solomon to hear his wisdom, which God had put in his heart. Each man brought his present: articles of silver and gold, garments, armor, spices, horses, and mules, at a set rate year by year. And Solomon gathered chariots and horsemen; he had one thousand four hundred chariots and twelve thousand horsemen, whom he stationed in the chariot cities and with the king at Jerusalem. The king made silver as common in Jerusalem as stones, and he made cedar trees as abundant as the sycamores which are in the lowland. Also Solomon had horses imported from Egypt and Keveh; the king's merchants bought them in Keveh at the current price. Now a chariot that was imported from Egypt cost six hundred shekels of silver, and a horse one hundred and fifty; and thus, through their agents, they exported them to all the kings of the Hittites and the kings of Syria."*
> – 1Ki 10:14-29

If you look carefully at those verses, you can see a lot of parallels, but of note to us right now are horses. In that list it was obvious that Solomon was multiplying horses, but did you know that this act was in direct violation of the Law that God had set for kings, which we find in Deut 17:16?

> *"But [the king] shall not multiply horses to himself, nor cause the people to return to Egypt, to the end that he should multiply horses: forasmuch as the LORD hath said unto you, 'Ye shall henceforth return no more that way.'" – Deu 17:16*

Also notice the chariots mentioned here. He had so many that he had chariot cities. The word for chariots there is extremely rare. In fact, there is no other time in the Old or New Testaments that this is used. No references in the LXX or anywhere else. There are plenty of mentions of chariots in the Bible, of course, but none of them are like this word. I will give you the definition from a standard lexicon.

> **G4480** α *rheda hred'-ah – Of Latin origin; a rheda, that is, four-wheeled carriage (wagon for riding): - chariot.*

That's right. This kind of chariot has four wheels. I don't have much to say about that except that I find the Bible to be fascinating.

"…slaves, and souls of men."

I think this last section may be unnecessarily confusing, especially this last part: **"souls of men."**

This same phrase is used in the Old Testament to refer to slaves. Not surprisingly, we find it in a passage about merchants. It says:

> *"Javan, Tubal, and Meshech, they were thy merchants: they traded the **persons** of men and vessels of brass in thy market." – Eze 27:13*

Authorized Version (KJV) Translation Count — Total: 753

AV — soul 475, life 117, person 29, mind 15, heart 15, creature 9, body 8, himself 8, yourselves 6, dead 5, will 4, desire 4, man 3, themselves 3, any 3, appetite 2, misc 47

Gesenius's Lexicon (Help)

נֶפֶשׁ with suff. נַפְשִׁי; plur. נְפָשׁוֹת (נְפָשִׁים once Eze.

The word "persons" there is the Hebrew word *nephesh* which is translated "souls" **475 times** in the Old Testament, but it is used in a variety of ways which you can see from this lexicon entry. I think that here in the Old Testament is the correct way to understand the idea of souls of men, and that is in terms of slaves. I'm sure the translators of Revelation simply rendered the word "*nephesh*" in its literal sense, "souls of men," even though it clearly has a much broader use in Scripture.

However, if that is true, it causes a bit of a conflict in Revelation 18:13, because we already have a word translated as "slaves." So am I saying that this verse should read they were selling "slaves and slaves?"

Let's look at the first word they have rendered as slaves.

This word is *soma* in the Greek it is used **146 times** in the New Testament, and it **never** means slaves other than this one time. The other 145 times it is rendered as bodies, either dead or living bodies. It is basically used the exact same way we use the word "body" in English.

So I think that this verse could have better been translated as "bodies and slaves."

I am not exactly sure how this will manifest during the antichrist's reign. I'm sure I could have un- earthed more interesting connections here, but at the very least, if we just take it at its face value and you consider that the antichrist will preside over the biggest genocide in history, you can start to make some guesses as to how this slavery could play out. To give an example of how much people will agree with this genocide, remember Jesus' words in the Olivet discourse:

> *"Now the brother shall betray the brother to death, and the father the son; and children shall rise up against their parents, and shall cause them to be put to death." – Mar 13:12*

So with such disregard for human life among the world at this time I don't know why we should expect them to care if these people, who they clearly hate and feel they are doing the world a favor by killing them, were used even as slaves.

(Rev 18:14)

And the fruits that thy soul lusted after are departed from thee, and all things which were dainty and goodly are departed from thee, and thou shalt find them no more at all.

All the delicious living that was described as being a part of the city of Mystery Babylon will cease when Judgment comes to it.

(Rev 18:15)

The merchants of these things, which were made rich by her, shall stand afar off for the fear of her torment, weeping and wailing.

"The merchants of these things…."

We have already mentioned that this seems to refute the idea that these merchants are a general term for the world economy or "Economic Babylon" as is often said by those who would seek to spiritualize the above passages.

Revelationcommentary.org notes:

> 1. *The merchants…mourning = echoes the situation of the kings above. Their reaction is the same as the kings.*
>
> 2. *Woe, woe, the great city = indicates that the lament of the*

merchants is the same as the kings'.

The Finality of Her Destruction

(Rev 18:16)

And saying, 'Alas, alas, that great city, that was clothed in fine linen, and purple, and scarlet, and decked with gold, and precious stones, and pearls!

"And saying, 'Alas, alas...'"

This is what the merchants will say when they watch her burn from afar off.

"...clothed in fine linen, and purple, and scarlet, and decked with gold, and precious stones, and pearls!"

This is the same description given of the harlot in Revelation 17:4.

They note again her clothing. It is fitting that the merchants refer to her by the items that they sold to her.

(Rev 18:17-18)

For in one hour so great riches is come to nought. And every shipmaster, and all the company in ships, and sailors, and as many as trade by sea, stood afar off, And cried when they saw the smoke of her burning, saying, 'What city is like unto this great city!

"For in one hour so great riches is come to nought...."

The suddenness of the city's destruction is expressed here. It is described as having occurred in one hour, although it is expressed as "one day" in other places in this chapter.

"And every shipmaster, and all the company in ships, and sailors, and as many as trade by sea..."

A third group of onlookers is introduced here. They are people who were on the sea for various reasons. We have already seen the kings and merchants doing basically this same thing, lamenting the city's destruction.

"...stood afar off..."

This is mentioned several times. Back in Rev 18:10, it seems to suggest that the reason they were standing far off is that they somehow feared they would be affected by the aftermath of the city's destruction.

"...and cried when they saw the smoke of her burning..."

This is the part that leads some to suggest that Mystery Babylon must be a port city, but this is not necessary. All that is said is that the smoke of its burning can be seen by the ships at sea.

I would say that it is, however, necessary that the smoke from the burning of Mystery Babylon must be able to be seen from the sea in order to be consistent with this face value hermeneutic.

Jerusalem is only 34 miles from the Mediterranean coast and its smoke could easily be seen from the sea. An example from modern times is that people reported being able to see the smoke and debris from the 911 attacks on the World Trade Center from 70 or more miles away.

This is a problem for those who insist that the actual city of Babylon is Mystery Babylon, because it is 300 miles from the nearest sea (the Persian Gulf), and a whopping 500 miles from the Mediterranean. It would be impossible for this to be applied to the literal city of Babylon.

Rome, by the way is also not a port city, being about 15 miles from the coast. This does not conflict with the fact that sea merchants bring goods to it. We see sea merchants bringing goods to Jerusalem in several places, notably the 1 Kings 10 passages referring to King Solomon, which we have already covered in depth.

"...saying, 'What *city is* like unto this great city!'"

The sailors here say this phrase hearkens back to the prophecies regarding the city of Tyrus or Tyre. We will be talking about this in depth in the next verse.

(Rev 18:19)

And they cast dust on their heads, and cried, weeping and wailing, saying, Alas, alas, that great city, wherein were made rich all that had ships in the sea by reason of her costliness! for in one hour is she made desolate.

This verse has some striking parallels to a passage in the Old Testament, which refers to the destruction of the merchant city of Tyrus. It says in Ezekiel 27:30-31:

> *"And shall cause their voice to be heard against thee, and **shall cry bitterly**, and shall **cast up dust upon their heads**, they shall wallow themselves in the ashes: And they shall make themselves utterly bald for thee, and gird them with sackcloth, and they shall <u>weep</u> for thee with bitterness of heart and bitter wailing." – Eze 27:30-31*

This is especially interesting in light of the other parallels between the language of the fall of Tyrus or Tyre and Mystery Babylon. We have covered some of these parallels in previous verses.

I have found it interesting that the Bible seems to go out of its way at times to refer to the destruction of Tyrus, and to the destruction of Babylon in the passages about Mystery Babylon.

For instance, in the passages about the destruction of literal Babylon in Jeremiah 51, there are phrases like:

> *"O thou that **dwellest upon many waters**, abundant in treasures, thine end is come, and the measure of thy covetousness." – Jer*

51:13

This is a clear connection to Mystery Babylon, which is said to "sit on many waters" in Revelation 17. The angel later gives us an interpretation as to what the water represents:

> *"And he saith unto me, 'The waters which thou sawest, where the whore sitteth, are peoples, and multitudes, and nations, and tongues.'" – Rev 17:15*

As I was reflecting on the significance of these cities as they relate to one another, I remembered a very interesting fact. Satan is referred to as the "King of Tyre" and the "King of Babylon" in different places in Scripture. When we look at those Old Testament prophecies, we will see that they would start out talking about the kings of these places, but before it's over it is clear that the scope of the prophecy is far too big to simply be referring to these earthly kings. See *Isaiah 14:4-15* and *Ezekiel 28:12-17*.

(Rev 18:20)

Rejoice over her, thou heaven, and ye holy apostles and prophets; for God hath avenged you on her.

"...thou heaven..."

We see a picture of those in heaven asking to be avenged back in Revelation 6.

> *"And when he had opened the fifth seal, I saw under the altar the souls of them that were slain for the word of God, and for the testimony which they held: And they cried with a loud voice, saying, 'How long, O Lord, holy and true, dost thou not judge and avenge our blood on them that dwell on the earth?'" – Rev 6:9-10*

And in Revelation 19 we see a picture of their rejoicing:

> *"And after these things I heard a great voice of much people in*

heaven, saying, 'Alleluia; Salvation, and glory, and honour, and power, unto the Lord our God: For true and righteous are his judgments: for he hath judged the great whore, which did corrupt the earth with her fornication, and hath avenged the blood of his servants at her hand.'" – Rev 19:1-2

"...and ye holy apostles and prophets; for God hath avenged you on her..."

We will study this idea in depth when we look at the last verse in this chapter about the "prophets and apostles and all those slain on the earth." We will see that Jesus puts the blame for all of them on the city of Jerusalem. One example is in Matthew 23:35 where He says:

> *"That upon you may come all the righteous blood shed upon the earth, from the blood of righteous Abel unto the blood of Zacharias son of Barachias, whom ye slew between the temple and the altar." – Mat 23:35*

Notice that He said all the righteous blood is on them. Abel was not a Jew, nor a prophet, nor was he killed in Jerusalem, but his blood was on Jerusalem's head. We will look more at the context of this verse later on. We will also see that the OT prophets were indeed killed in Jerusalem according to Scripture.

(Rev 18:21)

And a mighty angel took up a stone like a great millstone, and cast it into the sea, saying, 'Thus with violence shall that great city Babylon be thrown down, and shall be found no more at all.

This is the verse that is the best argument against Mystery Babylon being the last days city of Jerusalem. I will discuss it in detail in the last section which is dedicated to objections to this theory.

The question is, if Jerusalem is **"found no more,"** then how do we explain the fact that Jerusalem is very much a part of the millennial and eternal kingdoms?

The short answer to this question is that in the detailed layouts of the millennial kingdom given to us by Ezekiel in the last 9 chapters of his book (40-48), we are told, among other details, the physical location of the city of Jerusalem during that time. Those who attempt to map all of Ezekiel's specifications come to various conclusions, but almost all of them agree that the Jerusalem of the future is not in the exact location of the present city. In addition, the millennial Jerusalem is nine times larger than the current city. Also, the temple is located outside the city, and it alone is bigger than the current city of Jerusalem. The millennial Jerusalem sits on a high plateau, and has two rivers flowing out of its east and west sides. Basically, it is a different place altogether.

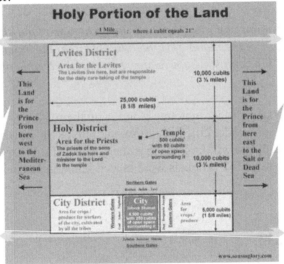

Some proposals for the location have been Bethlehem and Shiloh. Cameron in his paper "Zechariah in relation to Ezekiel 40-48"[9] makes a very compelling case that the new temple complex will be located at Shechem, a theory that I think is worth serious investigation. The point is that many put the Jerusalem of the future in a different physical location, not for any theological reasons, but because of careful study of Ezekiel's millennial blueprints.

For a more detailed discussion see the section on objections.

We will take these next two verses as a set.

(Rev 18:22-23)

And the voice of harpers, and musicians, and of pipers, and trumpeters, shall be heard no more at all in thee; and no craftsman, of whatsoever craft he be, shall be found any more in thee; and the sound of a millstone shall be heard no more at all in thee; And the light of a candle shall shine no more at all in thee; and the voice of the bridegroom and of the bride shall be heard no more at all in thee: for thy merchants were the great men of the earth; for by thy sorceries were all nations deceived.

This is an exact match with several verses in the book of Jeremiah. All of them together are a prophecy of the destruction of Jerusalem. One example is found in Jer 25:10:

> *"Moreover I will take from them the voice of mirth, and the voice of gladness, the voice of the **bridegroom**, and the voice of the bride, the **sound of the millstones**, and the **light of the candle**." – Jer 25:10*

Even more interesting to me is the reason that this particular judgment would come. About five chapters later the same prediction is made again, and it says:

> *"'**For the children of Judah** have done evil in my sight,' saith the LORD: 'They have **set their abominations in the house** which is called by my name, to pollute it…. Then will I cause to cease from the cities of Judah, and from the **streets of Jerusalem**, the **voice of mirth**, and the voice of gladness, the voice of the **bridegroom**, and the voice of the **bride**: for the **land shall be desolate**.'" – Jer 7:30, 34*

Jeremiah makes it clear what he means by the phrase "house called by my name" many times. One notable example, which was later quoted by Jesus, is when it says:

> *"Is **this house, which is called by my name**, become a den of robbers in your eyes? Behold, even I have seen it, saith the LORD."*
> *– Jer 7:11*

Now consider this – we have here the meaning of the "Abomination which causes Desolation" spoken of by Daniel. We see that the land will be made **desolate** because they sat an **abomination** in the **temple**.

This is pretty amazing, especially when you consider that our verse in Revelation 18:22-23 is referring to the aftermath of a city that does the same thing: worships the antichrist in the temple as if he were God (the Abomination that causes Desolation).

You have the exact same punishment described here, and for the exact same crime!

(Rev 18:24)

And in her was found the blood of prophets, and of saints, and of all that were slain upon the earth.

"...the blood of prophets..."

The killing of Old Testament prophets is many times blamed on the city of Jerusalem. There are many sayings from Jesus on this point.

> *"O **Jerusalem, Jerusalem, thou that killest the prophets**, and stonest them which are sent unto thee, how often would I have gathered thy children together, even as a hen gathereth her chickens under her wings, and ye would not!" – Mat 23:37*

Just before this statement Jesus explains it more in depth.

> *"Woe unto you, scribes and Pharisees, hypocrites! Because ye build the tombs of the prophets, and garnish the sepulchres of the righteous, And say, 'If we had been in the days of our fathers, we would not have been partakers with them in the blood of the*

*prophets.' Wherefore ye be witnesses unto yourselves, that **ye are the** **children of them which killed the prophets**. Fill ye up then the measure of your fathers. Ye serpents, ye generation of vipers, how can ye escape the damnation of hell? Wherefore, behold, I send unto you prophets, and wise men, and scribes: and some of them ye shall kill and crucify; and some of them shall ye scourge in your synagogues, and persecute them from city to city: **That upon you** **may come all the righteous blood shed upon the earth**, from the blood of righteous Abel unto the blood of Zacharias son of Barachias, whom ye slew between the temple and the altar." – Mat 23:29-35*

Jeremiah tried to warn them not to kill him for this reason.

*"But know ye for certain, that if ye put me to death, **ye shall surely** **bring innocent blood upon yourselves**, and **upon this city**, and **upon the inhabitants thereof**: for of a truth the LORD hath sent me unto you to speak all these words in your ears." – Jer 26:15*

In the book of Acts and in 1 Thessalonians, we see this same idea being taught:

*"**Which of the prophets have not your fathers persecuted?** and they have slain them which shewed before of the coming of the Just One; of whom ye have been now the betrayers and murderers..." – Act 7:52*

*"Who both killed the Lord Jesus, **and their own prophets**, and have persecuted us; and they please not God, and are contrary to all men..." – 1Th 2:15*

Jesus also tells a parable about this:

"And the husbandmen took his servants, and beat one, and killed another, and stoned another. Again, he sent other servants more than the first: and they did unto them likewise. But last of all he sent unto them his son, saying, 'They will reverence my son.' But when the husbandmen saw the son, they said among themselves, 'This is the heir; come, let us kill him, and let us seize on his inheritance.'" –

Mat 21:35-38

We also are told that the last prophets sent to Jerusalem (the two witnesses) will be killed in its streets:

> *"And their dead bodies shall lie in the street of the great city, which spiritually is called Sodom and Egypt, where also our Lord was crucified." – Rev 11:8*

"…and of saints…"

There have been many persecutions in history of Christians, but the worst one of all time, one that is yet to come, will, according to Jesus, have its epicenter in the city of Jerusalem.

> *"When ye therefore shall see the abomination of desolation, spoken of by Daniel the prophet, stand in the holy place, (whoso readeth, let him understand:) Then let them which be in Judaea flee into the mountains: Let him which is on the housetop not come down to take any thing out of his house: Neither let him which is in the field return back to take his clothes. And woe unto them that are with child, and to them that give suck in those days! But pray ye that your flight be not in the winter, neither on the sabbath day: **For then shall be great tribulation, such as was not since the beginning of the world to this time, no, nor ever shall be.** And except those days should be shortened, there should no flesh be saved: but for the elect's sake those days shall be shortened." – Mat 24:15-22*

Apparently, when the antichrist declares himself to be God, it will coincide with the order to kill "saints." Considering that order will first be given in Jerusalem, it will require those who wish to escape the initial wave to flee from the area very quickly.

The saints being killed by antichrist during this persecution is referenced again and again in Scripture. Here are just a few instances:

> *"I beheld, and the same horn made war with the saints, and prevailed against them…" – Dan 7:21*

"And it was given unto him to make war with the saints, and to overcome them: and power was given him over all kindreds, and tongues, and nations." – Rev 13:7

"And the dragon was wroth with the woman, and went to make war with the remnant of her seed, which keep the commandments of God, and have the testimony of Jesus Christ." – Rev 12:17

"...all that were slain upon the earth."

This is an interesting phrase. This tempts some to make everything in these two chapters allegorical, because, obviously, not everyone that was ever slain was slain in a particular city.

That is true. Nevertheless, Jesus says that Jerusalem is responsible for all the blood of the righteous.

*"That upon you may come all the righteous blood shed upon the earth, **from the blood of righteous Abel unto the blood of Zacharias son of Barachias**, whom ye slew between the temple and the altar." – Mat 23:35*

Again, notice the names he gives – Able the son of Adam, the first person ever slain in history! This is clearly used to emphasize that indeed He means ALL the righteous blood would be put on Jerusalem's hands.

An interesting section of the law in Deuteronomy describes how Israel should absolve itself from innocent blood if they see it happen. After a lengthy discussion about it, it concludes this way:

*"And they shall answer and say, 'Our hands have not shed this blood, neither have our eyes seen it. Be merciful, O LORD, unto thy people Israel, whom thou hast redeemed, and **lay not innocent blood unto thy people of Israel's charge.'** And the blood shall be forgiven them. So shalt thou put away the guilt of innocent blood from among you, when thou shalt do that which is right in the sight of the LORD." – Deu 21:7-9*

This practice that would have absolved them of innocent blood was obviously not kept. Another interesting section is when it describes why God destroyed Jerusalem in 2 Kings.

> *"And the LORD sent against him bands of the Chaldees, and bands of the Syrians, and bands of the Moabites, and bands of the children of Ammon, and sent them against Judah to destroy it, according to the word of the LORD, which he spake by his servants the prophets. Surely at the commandment of the LORD came this upon Judah, to remove them out of his sight, for the sins of Manasseh, according to all that he did;* ***And also for the innocent blood*** *that he shed:* ***for he filled Jerusalem with innocent blood; which the LORD would not pardon.*** *" – 2Ki 24:2-4*

This concludes the verse-by-verse portion of this book. I want to take this time to say that I assume that not everything I said here is correct. I am sure there are mistakes and false assumptions I have made along the way. This is a complicated study, and I'm sure my views will change slightly as people critique this. Feel free to contact me at my website:

www.BibleProphecyTalk.com.

Answers to Common Objections

The arguments I will be covering are as follows:

1.) How can Mystery Babylon be the last days city of Jerusalem if it is said to be "found no more" in Rev 18:21, and if we know that Jerusalem is a big part of the millennial reign and the eternal kingdom?

2.) When speaking of the Babylonian destruction of Jerusalem, Ezekiel 5:9 states: "And because of all your abominations I will do with you what I have never yet done, and the like of which I will never do again." Does this mean that Jerusalem will not be judged again?

3.) Is there a future judgment of Jerusalem in Scripture?

4.) Is this somehow anti-Semitic? How, if at all, does this affect one's views toward Israel?

5.) What about the 7 mountains?

Found no more?

One of the best arguments against the theory is rooted in the following verse:

> *"And a mighty angel took up a stone like a great millstone, and cast it into the sea, saying, 'Thus with violence shall that great city Babylon be thrown down, and **shall be found no more at all**.'" - Rev*

18:21

The argument is that Jerusalem can't be Mystery Babylon because it says that it shall be found "no more at all," and we know that Jerusalem is in the millennial reign. We also see the so-called "New Jerusalem" in the eternal kingdom. This is a very good argument, and it requires a very good answer. How can I say on the one hand that Jerusalem will be destroyed and be "found no more" and on the other hand say that it will be around forever?

I believe the answer lies in the last 8 chapters of the book of Ezekiel. There you will find one of the most intricate, detailed building plans for the Israel of the Millennium. It contains chapters and chapters of technical details regarding how Israel will be divided, about the new temple complex, and about Jerusalem and its surrounding areas. To say it is different than what we currently see in Israel is a bit of an understatement.

There are those who have taken all the technical specifications of things like the division of the land in the millennial reign and plotted it all on a map. The twelve tribes of Israel are given parallel rectangular allotments of land, one on top of the other, from the north border of Israel to the south, and each tribe's allotment extends along the entire east/west border of Israel. It really helps to see this all on a map to visualize what I'm saying.

In the middle of these allotments of land is a rectangular portion that Ezekiel calls the "Holy Portion." The priests and Levites who service the temple equally divide this land. There is some debate as to where exactly the temple is in this section. Some say it is in the middle of this land and others say that it

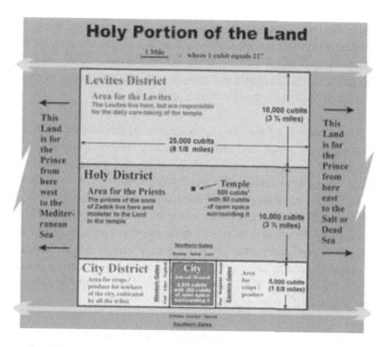

is just north of the city, but it doesn't appear to actually be in the city itself, which is very different from Jerusalem now.

In addition to several other things, the city of Jerusalem is most likely also very different in physical location during the millennium. We will talk about this in more detail later. For starters, it is perfectly square, and it is about nine times larger than the old city of Jerusalem is today. It has twelve gates – three on each side and it sits on a high plateau. It has two rivers that flow from it – the one on its east side flows to the Dead Sea and the one to its west flows all the way to the Mediterranean Sea. It is a different place; in fact, the last words in the book of Ezekiel are used to give this Jerusalem a different name. It says:

> *"It was round about eighteen thousand measures: and the name of the city from that day **shall be, The LORD is there**." - Eze 48:35*

This is sometimes transliterated "YHWH Shammah," which means, "The Lord is there. "

The temple, regardless of where it resides, is absolutely huge, and is a study that you may find very fascinating in and of itself. It mentions things like: "No wall of partition to exclude Gentiles and "no veil in the holy of holies." I found it interesting that the Temple Institute, that is the Jewish people in Israel who are seeking to rebuild the temple, said the following of this structure on their website templeinstitute.org:

> *"Many aspects of the Temple described by Ezekiel are difficult to comprehend, since that vision contains elements of prophetic insight which, in our generation, we do not have the spiritual or intellectual capacity to understand. For example, according to the prophecy of Ezekiel, the structure of the Third Temple will necessitate vast topographical changes in the environs of the Jerusalem. This Temple will differ drastically in size from its predecessors. According to Ezekiel's measurements, the new Temple will be so large that it will occupy the entire area of the city of Jerusalem. Ezekiel's prophecy explains that both the Temple Mount and the Mount of Olives will be enlarged and expanded in the future."*

The city of Jerusalem's actual location in the millennium is a matter of some debate. You should know that the people that I am about to cite have no theological reason for saying that the location of the Jerusalem in the Millennial period is in a different location than the present city of Jerusalem; they do not, as far as I know, consider Mystery Babylon to be the last days city of Jerusalem; they are simply trying to map out some of the details that Ezekiel gives in these 8 chapters.

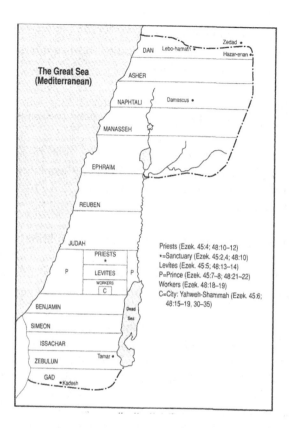

The International Standard Bible Encyclopedia gives two options based on the text, both of them south of Jerusalem. One of the possible locations is at Bethlehem and the other is a little further north, but still south of Jerusalem, at modern day Ramat Rahel.[10] Another researcher puts forward a good case for the millennial Jerusalem or "Yawheh Shammah" being located at Shiloh, and another possibility that Cameron in his paper makes a case for is Shechem.[11]

Even if the new city of Yahweh Shammah sat right on top of the old Jerusalem, we must at least conclude that it is nine times larger than the current city; therefore it obviously does not contain the same physical landmarks and boundaries as the previous Jerusalem. And we know from various places in the Bible that it will sit on a large raised platform – a long plateau that makes it visible from a very long way off. I have already mentioned that two rivers flow from it on either side, so we know that it's geographically not the same place either. We start to get the idea that God will willingly call this city Jerusalem regardless of its not having the same borders, or geography, or physical location.

Take for example the New Jerusalem of the eternal kingdom: it is called Jerusalem as well, despite it being a whopping 1500 miles long.

Some groups, such as Amillennialists, try to make the New Jerusalem of the eternal kingdom (that is the time period after the millennial reign) equal with Ezekiel's Jerusalem based on the fact that they both have twelve gates named for the twelve tribes, and a few other attributes.

The differences, however, are far greater than the similarities. For example, consider the size: the New Jerusalem is about 1500 miles wide, which would encompass most of the countries in the Mid East. This is compared to Ezekiel's 9-mile-square city, and the current one-mile old city.

Some other notable differences are that the New Jerusalem comes down from heaven (21:2) and Ezekiel's Jerusalem is located in Israel on Earth (40:2). There is no temple in the New Jerusalem. It says that God and the Lamb are its Temple (21:22), while the temple in the book of Ezekiel is huge and is located north of the city (40:2). There is no sin; nothing impure will ever enter the New Jerusalem (21:27), while daily sin offerings are made in the Temple in Ezekiel's version (45:13-15, 17). There is no more death in the New Jerusalem (21:4), while there is still death in the book of Ezekiel (44:25 and also Isa 65:20). There are no natural beings in the New Jerusalem, only the perfected (21:27), yet there are natural beings in Ezekiel (46:16).

I mention all this to be able to say the following: God has no problem calling the New Jerusalem "Jerusalem" even though it clearly isn't tied to the exact place that the current Jerusalem is, and the same is true with the city called Yahweh Shammah. It can be the Millennial Jerusalem even though the old location has apparently been destroyed.

In fact, I think that the judgment of the old city of Jerusalem described in the following passages actually creates the topographical changes such as the plateau, and the river that will run through the land.

"And there were voices, and thunders, and lightnings; and there was

a great earthquake, such as was not since men were upon the earth, so mighty an earthquake, and so great. And the great city was divided into three parts, and the cities of the nations fell: and great Babylon came in remembrance before God, to give unto her the cup of the wine of the fierceness of his wrath."– Rev 16:18-19

As I noted in 17:11, this verse actually contrasts the so-called "Great city" (Mystery Babylon) with the "cities of the nations." This is a way to designate "The Great city" as a non-Gentile city.

I would also make the case that the reason the Lord splits the Mount of Olives, despite much confusion on this issue, is to make an escape route out of the old city of Jerusalem for the faithful remnant of Jews who are alive after the time of Jacob's Trouble. Consider in context, this passage in the Book of Zechariah:

*"And his feet shall stand in that day upon the mount of Olives, **which is before Jerusalem on the east**, and the mount of Olives shall cleave in the midst thereof toward the east and toward the west, and there shall be a very great valley; and half of the mountain shall remove toward the north, and half of it toward the south. **And ye shall flee to the valley of the mountains; for the valley of the mountains shall reach unto Azal:** yea, ye shall flee, like as ye fled from before the earthquake in the days of Uzziah king of Judah: and the LORD my God shall come, and all the saints with thee." – Zec 14:4-5*

Why is the Lord getting the faithful to flee from Jerusalem with such extravagant measures in this moment of triumph? It is because of the earthquake that is about to split the city in three parts described in Revelation 16.

Essentially, the old city of Jerusalem will be judged for its taking for itself the king known as antichrist. Among other things, it will be found no more. But a much more glorious city of Jerusalem with a different size, location, and topography will continue at least until the point of the eternal kingdom, when once again a different kind of Jerusalem will overshadow the former.

He Wont Do It Again

The next biblical objection to this theory is found in Ezekiel 5, verse 9, where it says:

> *"And because of all your abominations I will do with you what I have never yet done, and the like of which **I will never do again.**" – Eze 5:9*

In context, this prophecy was about the Babylonian conquest of Jerusalem. People will say, "How can Jerusalem be judged again if God said that he would never do the like again to Jerusalem?"

First of all, God does not say that He will never judge Israel or Jerusalem again; He says he will never do it again **like** He has done with the Babylonians. A similar promise can be seen in the book of Genesis:

> *"And I will establish my covenant with you; neither shall all flesh be cut off any more by the waters of a flood; neither shall there any more be a flood to destroy the earth." – Gen 9:11*

In these passages, God does not say He won't judge them at all anymore, only that He won't judge them in that way again. In fact, there are explicit promises to judge both Jerusalem and the world again, as we will see later on, albeit not by means of a flood.

The second point that I would like to make is that this passage in Eze 5:9 is difficult for all commentators regardless of their theological positions because the destruction of Jerusalem in 70 AD and the destruction of Jerusalem by the Babylonians were actually very similar events in the way that they were destroyed.

> They both were besieged by their enemies, creating terrible conditions of famine and disease inside the city before the enemies ever got in.
>
> In both cases, those who didn't die from disease or famine died from the sword, just as prophesied in Ezekiel 5:12.

And in both cases a remnant that was not killed was scattered, creating a diaspora, just as prophesied in Ezekiel 5:9.

It is such a close fit that this issue has become synonymous with the idea of a double fulfillment of prophecy. In fact, if you look up dual fulfillment on Wikipedia, you will see that this is one of the three examples that are given for dual prophecies in the Bible. I would submit that there are many more, but I wanted to point out that these destructions are very similar.

This similarity gives Bible scholars a difficult time in light of the passage in question, Eze 5:9, but ironically, it poses no problem to the theory that Mystery Babylon is Jerusalem. In fact, I would submit that the destruction of Jerusalem that I am talking about, the one described in the Mystery Babylon passages, is the only destruction that can be said to be 180 degrees different from the previous destructions of Jerusalem by Nebuchadnezzar in 597 BC and Titus in 70 AD.

For instance, four times in Revelation 18 it mentions that the destruction of Mystery Babylon occurs in "one day" or "one hour" (Rev 18:8, 18:10, 18:17, Rev 18:19). This is in sharp contrast to the previous long and drawn out sieges of Jerusalem.

This destruction of Mystery Babylon is accomplished by a combination of things:

> The biggest earthquake of all time

> Great hail from heaven

> The kings of the earth, who burn her with fire.

In fact, fire in various forms is mentioned another three times. And while fire is also mentioned as part of the destruction of Jerusalem by Nebuchadnezzar, and in a lesser way during the 70 AD destruction, the fires in those cases were set after the conquest was over, and no mention of death by fire was recorded. This is in contrast to the text mentioning fires four times as the primary agent of destruction of Mystery Babylon. In addition, Ezekiel makes it clear that the methods God used for the previous destructions were sword, famine, and pestilence, and there can be no doubt that that is where the destruction came from in the previous cases.

This "one day" or "one hour" destruction of Mystery Babylon and its close proximity to the millennium in Revelation 18 also has no room for the scattering to the winds of the remnant of the Jews as was the case in 597 BC and 70 AD, which is also an expressly stated part of the judgment of the previous destructions in Eze 5:10. So the future judgment of Jerusalem will be nothing like the previous destructions of Jerusalem, and I see no conflict with Ezekiel 5:9 and the future judgment of Jerusalem whatsoever.

Before I start on the next objection, I would like to appeal to those of you who have read the Old Testament extensively and remind you that all throughout Israel's biblical history they have desired a king who would look the part and who would basically give them what they wanted – that is the conquering Messiah who would deliver them from their current enemies, a king who would fulfill the prophecies of putting Jerusalem in the top spot of the cities of the earth. Now, of course, this will actually happen in the millennial reign. Jerusalem will be the city that rules the nations of the earth. We know this for the same reason that the Jews are expecting this because the Scriptures, like Ezekiel, say it will happen.

We must understand that one of the main reasons that many Jewish leaders rejected Jesus at the time was because He didn't seem to be fulfilling that conquering part of the Messianic prophecies at His first coming. He fulfilled the prophecies of the suffering Messiah of Isaiah 53, which we are so thankful for.

In fact, even His disciples didn't quite get this at the time. They seemed to think that at some point He would start conquering the enemies of Israel and establish Jerusalem as the world capital. Even after He rose from the dead, and just before He ascended into heaven, it says in Acts 1: 6-7:

> *"When they therefore were come together, they asked of him, saying,*
> **'Lord, wilt thou at this time restore again the kingdom to Israel?'**
> *And he said unto them, 'It is not for you to know the times or the*
> *seasons, which the Father hath put in his own power.'" – Act 1:6-7*

What I am saying is that Satan knows all of this as well. He knows that they are waiting on a messiah- king who makes Jerusalem the capital city of the world in fulfillment of the messianic prophecies. The reason we see the antichrist being so tied to Jerusalem in the last days is because he plans on making use of this thirst for a conquering messiah-king who will make them the center of all the world's religion and economy. And he will in fact seem to deliver on this promise for a time.

The next argument against this theory is a more general one. It is a kind of belief that Jerusalem is not going to be judged any more and that Jerusalem is a kind of city that will forever be free from judgment since the Jews are back in the land.

However, there are many passages that speak of a future eschatological judgment of Israel that contains elements that are beyond the scope of any previous judgment.

When a prophecy fits this description, it almost always speaks of it in the same way, using similar vocabulary and themes. It speaks of a fiery trial, a purification of Israel that immediately precedes its ultimate redemption, and its final atonement for past sins. This final reconciliation for sins is typified in the completion of the 70 weeks of Daniel.

A good example of this fiery judgment just before reconciliation is found in Isaiah 4 just before passages that are widely considered to be talking of the millennial reign. The Millennial period seems to have the prerequisite of purifying judgment by fire for the Jews.

> *"When the Lord shall have washed away the filth of the daughters of Zion, and shall have purged the blood of Jerusalem from the midst thereof by the spirit of judgment, and by the spirit of burning. And the LORD will create upon every dwelling place of mount Zion, and upon her assemblies, a cloud and smoke by day, and the shining of a flaming fire by night: for upon all the glory shall be a defence. And there shall be a tabernacle for a shadow in the daytime from the heat, and for a place of refuge, and for a covert from storm and from rain." – Isa 4:4-6*

We see similar language in the post-exilic prophets. The reason why their being post-Babylonian exile is important is that one cannot say that the following were prophecies of Babylon's destruction of Jerusalem.

For example, a post-exilic prophecy that wasn't fulfilled completely by 70AD is found in Zechariah 13:8- 9:

> *"'In the whole land," declares the LORD 'two-thirds will be struck down and perish; yet one-third will be left in it. This third I will put into the fire; I will refine them like silver and test them like gold. They will call on my name and I will answer them; I will say, 'They are my people, and they will say, 'The LORD is our God.'"*

Also:

> *"At that time Michael shall stand up, The great prince who stands watch over the sons of your people; And there shall be a time of trouble, Such as never was since there was a nation, Even to that time. And at that time your people shall be delivered, Every one who is found written in the book." – Daniel 12:1*

This fiery refining just before their redemption is the time spoken of as the time of Jacob's trouble, which begins with the eschatological Day of the Lord and ends with the end of the 70th week. It is often missed that the one who troubles Jacob in this time, is God himself, even though He may do this through various agents. He will refine one third of national Israel during this time of judgment. This one third of national Israel will come to know Jesus as Messiah, possibly through the ministry of the two witnesses, but either way they will help to populate the millennial kingdom that we saw earlier in the charts.

So yes, Israel will be judged for its sins, particularly their embracing of the antichrist. They are not going to be exempt, and the teaching that they are is simply not biblical or logical.

Anti-semitic?

Some people wonder if the interpretation that the last days city of Jerusalem is Mystery Babylon is in some way anti-Semitic. Or they will wonder exactly how we should view modern day Israel and Jerusalem in light of this information.

The short answer is that this is not anti-Semitic. Reading about Israel's falling short in the OT is not an anti-Semitic activity and neither is this. But more to the point, this is not a theory about current Jerusalem but a future one that we have not seen yet. And when it comes, their future sin of worshiping and promoting the antichrist is really no different than the rest of the world's sin which is the exact same thing. Their future sin is compounded by their fierce promotion of the antichrist as messiah and their having known the true God previously, but this embracing of the antichrist is not unique to them. It is a sin that the entire unsaved world will share in.

As far as how we should view Israel in light of this information, I think anyone who knows me or my previous work, knows that I tend to default or err in support of Israel. But that does not mean that I think they can do no wrong or are on the right side of every political issue. I think we are instructed to pray for them and preach to them and love them.

What about the Seven Hills?

See **(Rev 17:9-10)...p.34**

What about Abaddon?

Because I spent a lot of time in verse 8 making the case that the antichrist coming out of the abyss was a reference to his apparent resurrection, I need to address another reference to the Abyss in the book of Revelation in order to avoid confusion.

It is my conviction that the antichrist is **not** being referred to in Revelation 9 during the fifth trumpet even though the "bottomless pit" or "Abyss" is mentioned there as well. In this case I think it is referring to the place that certain demonic sprits are being imprisoned.

> *"And they had a king over them, which is the angel of the bottomless pit, whose name in the Hebrew tongue is Abaddon, but in the Greek tongue hath his name Apollyon." – Rev 9:11*

First, it should be noted that this angel is nowhere said to be, itself, **from** the bottomless pit, or having come out of the bottomless pit. It is simply ruling over and directing the beings that do come out of it and making sure that they do what they are supposed to do.

In fact Revelationcommentary.org notes:

> *"The angel of the abyss is identified as king over the horrible locust-like-creatures. The exact identity of this angel is not certain. The particular grammatical construction (Genitive of subordination) here indicates that this angel is over the bottomless pit. It does not say that the angel is from the bottomless pit."*

There are many reasons that I don't see these two figures, the angel called "Abaddon" and the beast we know as antichrist, as being the same.

A few reasons would be that this passage in Revelation 9 would constitute the **only** time in Scripture that the antichrist is referred to as an angel, and not a man; it would also be the **only** verse in Scripture that connects the antichrist with things like the fifth trumpet, or ruling over a five month long physical torment of only wicked people, or his name being Destroyer (the translation of the titles). It seems much more likely that this passage should simply be taken at face value.

The fifth trumpet here, about the locusts being let out to torment those who do not have the seal of God for five months seems to be no different than the other trumpet and bowl judgments in the sense that they have mostly godly angels overseeing the destruction of the wicked.

I see no reason that this should be taken out of the context of the simplicity and **limited nature** of the fifth trumpet. All that happens in the fifth trumpet is that the destroying angel (this is what Abaddon and Apollyon mean) oversees the entities that torment the earth in an event that lasts for five months and five months alone. That's it. There is no other mention of this angel having any further purpose in the end-times scenario.

It may very well be that the entities that are let out of the abyss are demonic spirits, but the angel who rules over those spirits seems to make sure that they only target the ungodly, and only for five months.

The function of this angel is like the "destroying angel" of Exodus in the sense that the godly are passed over to kill the ungodly, and almost no one disagrees that in Exodus it was an angel of God, if not God himself, designated as "the destroyer."

Or consider 1 Chronicles 21:15, where we see an unambiguous case of a godly angel designated as a "destroying" angel. This is where David had sinned in the taking of the census.

> *"And **God sent an angel** unto Jerusalem to **destroy** it: and as he was **destroying**, the LORD beheld, and he repented him of the evil, and said to the **angel that destroyed**, It is enough, stay now thine hand. And the angel of the LORD stood by the threshing floor of Ornan the Jebusite. And David lifted up his eyes, and saw the angel of the LORD stand between the earth and the heaven, having a drawn sword in his hand stretched out over Jerusalem." – 1Ch 21:15-16*

For more Bible prophecy podcasts, Videos and Books from Chris White go to

www.BibleProphecyTalk.com

---

[1] http://www.vatican.va/archive/ENG0839/_P12J.HTM

[2] Jesus gives Jerusalem the blame for the killing of all the prophets (Mat 23:30-35). It does not mean that all prophets were necessarily killed in Jerusalem, although most, if not all of them were according to Scripture and tradition.

[3] Adam Clarke, The Holy Bible containing the Old and New Testaments, (1823), Vol 6, p. 950.

[4] Arthur W. Pink, A. W. Pink's Studies In the Scriptures - 1922-23, Volume 1 of 17, (Sovereign Grace Publishers Inc, 2001), p. 211.

[5] *The prophetic perfect tense is a verb tense that some claim is used by the prophets in the Hebrew Bible. This literary technique refers to future events in the past tense, known as deictic center shift. http://en.wikipedia.org/wiki/Prophetic_perfect_tense*

[6] *Gregory H. Harris, Can Satan Raise the Dead?, Toward a Biblical View of the Beast?s Wound, TMSJ 18/1 (Spring 2007) 23-41, http://www.tms.edu/tmsj/tmsj18b.pdf*

[7] *Walvoord, John F. Bible.org, "The Fall of Babylon." https://bible.org/seriespage/18-fall-babylon.*

[8] *John Kitto, and William Lindsay Alexander, Encyclopedia of Biblical Literature, Part 1, (Kessinger Publishing, LLC, 2003), p.110.*

[9] *C. MacKay, "Zechariah in Relation to Ezekiel 40-48" Evangelical Quarterly 40, 1968 CAMERON MACKAY, http://www.biblicalstudies.org.uk/pdf/eq/1968-4_197.pdf*

[10] *Geoffrey W Bromiley, International Standard Bible Encyclopedia: E-J, (Eerdmans Pub Co,), p. 261*

[11] C. MacKay, "Zechariah in Relation to Ezekiel 40-48" Evangelical Quarterly 40, 1968